DreamBabe

DreamBabe

Understanding Dreams—and Using Them to Make Your Dreams Come True

Barrie Dolnick

NEW AMERICAN LIBRARY

New American Library
Published by New American Library, a division of
Penguin Group (USA) Inc., 375 Hudson Street,
New York, New York 10014, USA
Penguin Group (Canada), 10 Alcorn Avenue, Toronto,
Ontario M4V 3B2, Canada (a division of Pearson Penguin Canada Inc.)
Penguin Books Ltd., 80 Strand, London WC2R 0RL, England
Penguin Ireland, 25 St. Stephen's Green, Dublin 2,
Ireland (a division of Penguin Books Ltd.)
Penguin Group (Australia), 250 Camberwell Road, Camberwell,
Victoria 3124, Australia (a division of Pearson Australia Group Pty. Ltd.)
Penguin Books India Pvt. Ltd., 11 Community Centre, Panchsheel Park,
New Delhi - 110 017, India
Penguin Group (NZ), Cnr Airborne and Rosedale Roads, Albany,
Auckland 1310, New Zealand (a division of Pearson New Zealand Ltd.)
Penguin Books (South Africa) (Pty.) Ltd., 24 Sturdee Avenue,
Rosebank, Johannesburg 2196, South Africa

Penguin Books Ltd, Registered Offices:
80 Strand, London WC2R 0RL, England

First published by New American Library,
a division of Penguin Group (USA) Inc.

First Printing, October 2004
10 9 8 7 6 5 4 3 2 1

LIBRARY OF CONGRESS CATALOGING-IN-PUBLICATION DATA:
Dolnick, Barrie.
DreamBabe : understanding dreams, and using them to make your dreams come true / Barrie Dolnick.
p. cm.
ISBN 0-451-21302-5 (trade pbk.)
1. Dreams. 2. Dream interpretation. I. Title: Dream Babe. II. Title.
BF175.5.D74D65 2004
154.6'3—dc22 2004006740

Set in Village
Designed by Jennifer Ann Daddio

Printed in the United States of America

Was it a vision, or a waking dream?

Fled is that music:—do I wake or sleep?

—KEATS, "*ODE TO A NIGHTINGALE*"

Acknowledgments

Thanks to the many dreamers who shared their dreams with me, among them Amie, Ann, Daniel, Guler, Jen, JillEllyn, Kathryn, Lis, Melissa, Monique, Sandy, Shelly, and Valerie.

In every enterprise, I greatly appreciate the support of my family—my husband, Gero; my daughter, Elisabeth; and my sisters, Randy, Amy, and Carol; and, of course, Mom.

I would also like to express gratitude to my teachers and friends—Cheryl, Heidi, Jennie, Joelle, Julia, Julie, Liz, Rachel, Sarah, Sheila, and Susan.

Last, I thank my agent, Alan Nevins, for his hard work, sense of humor, and faith in my outlandish ideas, and Tracy Bernstein, an amazing editor with vision, patience, and grace.

Contents

DreamBabe

Introduction

How often has one of your friends ruined a conversation by saying, "I had the weirdest dream . . ." and proceeding to describe (in lengthy detail) a scenario that seems totally irrelevant to your life and probably to hers, too? And how often have you heard yourself say and do that very same thing? Frankly, we all do it, and we can't help it. Dreams can be totally weird, sometimes scary, once in a while awesome (then it's hard to wake up), and even sexy (who can say no to that?). Dreams are very cool. They're your own independent films, and they have an enormous impact on your life—even (I'm totally serious) if you can't remember them.

If you're familiar with popular psychology, you'll

know that dreams are often considered a way for your unconscious mind to work out issues, fears, and problems. Whether you're stressed by your mother, your career, or your love life, your dreams can reflect anxieties or fears you feel on a deep level. Most of the time your dreams are hard to interpret—after all, what does diving into a ten-foot chocolate cake have to do with your boyfriend? (How about letting go and indulging in pleasure?) It takes a certain amount of knowledge, practice, and even humor to figure out what your dreams mean.

I once had a client who was unhappy in her marriage and wanted to find a new guy. I told her about a technique she could use to dream about having an affair (it's safe and you can't be sued for adultery!) to see what her dream might tell her. Sometimes a good dream can make you feel better than anything in waking life.

She tried this technique and told me that she had a weird dream—about lots of mailboxes. She was clearly frustrated that, rather than an erotic dream, she got a postal dream—a seemingly unlikely dream response. I couldn't help laughing and asked her if she knew what the slang word "box" meant. She looked puzzled for a second, then nodded. "It's slang for 'vagina.' " I told her to think about it. Mailboxes—*male* boxes. She was looking for an affair and her dream said there were lots of "male boxes" around; that is, there were opportunities for sex, but not for love.

Yes, dreams are punny, as well as weird.

There are many kinds of dreams, all offering you some insight into your world. Psychoanalysts like to use dreams to uncover issues that might be making you unhappy. But dreams aren't just for interpreting your complex psyche. They are also psychic energy and can be used to create new things in your life. Dreams can be empowering; they can help you work out some problem or difficulty. You can even consciously use your dreams to improve yourself, your skills, and your creativity. How about working on your abs in dream space? Why not?

There are many people who actually dream with purpose, using their dreams to inspire their creative lives, to explore new ideas, and to invent new things. Basically, dreams represent a huge potential of creative and psychic space where you can play, work, and create. But you have to know how to do it.

The next time someone tells you about her

dreams, you'll be able to give it right back to her, to decode it, to offer insight and even advice. Dreams aren't as irrelevant as you think, and they're much more powerful—so much so that they can influence your life and even make it better. So when you wonder if your dreams can come true, you can answer that one for yourself.

Dream Space

Dreams seem to take place in your head, in your imagination, where, though they aren't real, your mind makes them seem real for that moment.

How would you feel if you knew that dream space was actually a *real* space—a reality totally different from our daily life, but a reality nonetheless? Hold on to your pillows, kids, it's true. Dreams take place in different realms, and they aren't all in your head.

Yes, for the most part, you create your dream—though I know that can be very hard to remember when you're being chased by wild animals. You are, in fact, pretty much in charge of what happens. Where your dream occurs is a psychic place that consists of real energy—creative energy, emotional energy, passionate energy—but not physical energy. This is why you can die in a dream and still wake up. This is why dreams seem so real but aren't manifested in daily life. And this is why it's great to learn to dream with purpose, so you can use this amazing, resourceful space to explore a whole new reality.

Granted, the idea of a dream realm is hard to grasp. How can you call something real if it's not physical? Isn't it just your imagination? You could argue that dreams are just fantasies and not real at all—until you have one of those knockdown and blow-you-away dreams that you could swear was completely real, totally powerful, and just the tiniest bit prophetic. Then you know that your brain isn't just killing time by making mini-me movies.

If you prefer to remain a skeptic, please do, but you will, at some point, dream something powerful and know that your dream wasn't just a coincidence.

If you do accept the fact that there is indeed a dream realm, you're ready to roll. There are many different kinds of dreams—anxiety dreams (nothing like waking up after one of those!), dreams that are right out of some sci-fi movie, dreams that make you feel euphoric (you know what I'm talking about), and dreams that simply freak you out. In your dreams you're actually visiting different realms—different psychic spaces that allow you to work out problems or simply experiment with ideas. You can heal lots of issues in your life while you're dreaming.

Dreaming isn't just one state, just as waking life isn't one state. You're reading right now, but later you'll eat something, maybe talk on the phone, go to the gym, see friends—these are all different states of your waking life. In dreams, you get a chance to experience even more activities than when you're awake.

Sleeping opens your psychic state, and dreaming permits you to explore many realms that exist outside your physical reality.

Dream space has no boundaries because it is an energetic, not physical, domain. Dream space is extremely psychically attuned. Even if in everyday life you feel about as psychic as a bagel, in dream space you're directly hooked up to this amazing energy of foresight, knowledge, and creativity. This is why it is so great to learn how to use your dreams.

Because dream space is so psychically open, many people are visited by dead loved ones during dreams. It's easier for spirits to contact you while you're asleep because you're on a more psychic, more available plane.

A few years ago, my mother dreamed that her mother, who had died a few years earlier, was in the kitchen of her house, in a frenzy of cooking. Lydia, my grandmother's late sister, was with her, also bustling around ferociously preparing food. My mother heard them saying that they had to hurry, because Lou, their brother, was coming over. They wanted everything to be ready for him.

My mom reported her dream to me the next morning. Later that day, Lou died, no doubt joining his sisters in the feast they had prepared for him in the dream realm.

This was a prophetic dream, of course. My mother's dream realm was able to receive this information, although she didn't know it at the time. How often have you doubted something you dreamed and then watched "real life" conjure it up? It's hard to know when a dream is prophecy or something your psyche is doing to work out solutions. Sometimes, dreams serve more than one purpose.

The most important thing to remember is that dreams are completely different from waking reality. If you let go of the need to make sense of everything, you'll be able to learn more from your dreams. This sounds contradictory, but you'll soon learn that dream language is in your own, private code. It may seem tough to crack at first, but you'll be able to decipher it soon enough.

The Science of Sleep and the Nature of Dreams

It's important to remember that sleeping is a critical regenerative state for your body and that you need to sleep in order to be physically well and mentally alert. Most scientists believe dreams occur in sleep only sporadically throughout the night, during a period of sleep called Rapid Eye Movement, or REM. If you've ever seen a cat or dog dreaming, you know what this is. I like to watch our cat dream—her whiskers and her tail twitch and her eyes move back and forth behind her lids. She is no doubt frantically pursuing some prey in her dream space.

We aren't much different. When we dream, our eyes move and sometimes our bodies twitch. But our brains are smart enough to keep us from really moving, running, or reacting to our dreams. We dream we're up and about, we feel we're up and about, but our brains keep us immobile so we don't act on them while asleep. It's really remarkable how our bodies go into such a deeply restful state while our psyches are busy exploring and creating fabulous scenarios. You can even wake up rested after a big night of dream partying.

Your dream time, REM sleep, occurs for different lengths of time and at varying intervals. It's different for each of us. The most often recalled REM sleep is the period right before you wake up, the last dream of your night. That dream is the easiest to recall, and in my experience, it's the most powerful dream as well.

If you want to practice remembering your last dream, don't wake up by an alarm. Let yourself wake up naturally and stay in bed for a few moments, letting your mind drift to the dream you just had.

But I Don't Dream

I hear this all the time, especially from people who have young kids. Yes, you do. Maybe you don't remember your dreams, but you have them. If people are actually deprived of dreaming in laboratory-controlled sleep tests, they make up for it the next night.

Someone *consistently* deprived of REM sleep can get depressed, lose concentration, and even exhibit psychotic behavior.

Note: Certain sleep disorders can prevent REM sleep. Among them are sleep apnea and insomnia. If you suffer from these ailments, consult a doctor. You not only need your sleep—you need your dreams.

Dreaming History

Dreams have been a subject of great interest and discussion for as long as humans have been able to communicate with one another. Dreams were held sacred in Mesopotamia, the so-called cradle of civilization, and societies such as the Babylonians, Sumerians, and Egyptians considered dreams highly relevant and prophetic. Most of these cultures appointed people, like priests or oracles, to dream for advice regarding the society's welfare—no doubt a career some of us would be happy to have today.

While the interpretation of dream symbols varied across those ancient cultures, it was commonly accepted that dreams were powerful and important.

Dreams are discussed throughout both the Old and New Testaments beginning in Genesis (remember Jacob's dream of the ladder with angels climbing up and down).

Dreams maintained a significant role in religious and cultural life until translations of the Bible from Greek and Hebrew into Latin gave way to (some say) deliberate mistranslation, equating dreams with witchcraft. To interpret dreams and consider them divine messages was suddenly unholy and perceived to be tainted or sinful. People continued to dream, of course, but, dream interpretation lost favor while superstitions and judgments about dreams thrived.

The church's powerful stance against dream interpretation combined with the growing popularity of scientific thought pretty much put dream work on hold. For hundreds of years, dreams were considered gibberish your brain concocted while you were sleeping. This was only official doctrine, of course. Your great-great-great-grandmother and her ancestors probably never stopped thinking about and interpreting their dreams. Ancient habits die hard!

Dream interpretation and the entire language of dreams were revived in the early twentieth century, when Dr. Sigmund Freud reasserted their validity.

As the father of psychoanalysis and psychotherapy, Freud championed dream interpretation, contending that dreams come from the unconscious self. He theorized that dreams are expressions of "wish fulfillment" and that they express important information about our deeper issues and conflicts. He wasn't convinced that we all use the same symbols in our dreams, but in order to prove his point, he established certain guidelines for what seemed to be common dream language. While Freud's work established a foundation upon which more modern theories of psychology and dream interpretation are based, he didn't have any idea how to deal with women and their dreams. To be fair, he had a lot on his plate just establishing his field, and at the time women were considered less important than men. You've heard of "penis envy"? That's Freud. As I said, he didn't understand women. Freud's interpretation of many common dream symbols have sexual connotations—buildings are penises, caves are vaginas, etc. He basically brought everything in life down to sex. His approach may or may not work for you.

Not everyone agrees with Freud's symbols and their meanings, of course. Carl Jung, who studied with Freud, felt that Freud's dream theory was too limiting and moved dream interpretation into a broader direction. Jung proposed that dreams are both an expression of your unconscious self, or personality, as well as an expression of what he called "the collective unconscious," which is basically a shared realm of world experience. It's in this collective unconscious that dreams provide us with basic symbols for interpretation, which Jung labeled "universally accepted archetypes." In this view, the collective unconscious is a conceptual archive of all beliefs in all history; in this unconscious, universal realm, there are some dream symbols that we all encounter. Jung didn't dismiss the idea of psychic phenomenon, but science was more important to him. We owe a lot to Jung and his maverick efforts to open up dream work to examination and consideration, not to mention his work in furthering psychoanalysis and its usefulness in our society.

But Jung died in 1961, and despite the popularity of psychoanalysis, dream work didn't broadly catch on until the 1970s. Dreams are now explored professionally both for analysis, to understand ourselves and work out issues, as well as for psychic and spiritual content that can offer healing and karmic evolution.

You can decide for yourself what you believe your dreams to be. You already participate in dreaming; now it's up to you to use those dreams. Wisely.

Tracking Freud's Influence

There are many "classic" dreams, those that most of us experience in one form or another.

A "teeth" dream is common to most of us.

I used to have the classic teeth-falling-out dream, which has morphed into a gum-chewing dream. I'm chewing gum and the gum starts to take over my mouth, filling in between my teeth, going down my throat. I try to pull the gum out, kind of like in a cartoon. I pull and pull and pull, but it keeps choking me. Needless to say, I don't like to chew gum (never did much) anymore.

—Kayla, 38

Freud's interpretation of losing teeth (or, in this case, gum choking the dreamer) would have been about castration (he was pretty intractable on the relationship of symbols to sexual meaning). Since women don't have a lot to fear when it comes to castration, it's not that plausible—or at least not that obvious. Looking more closely, you can see that losing teeth is like losing your "edge," your ability to bite, losing a way of defending yourself. Choking on too much gum also blocks your ability to speak and communicate. Kayla's dreams were telling her that she lacked the ability to express herself and to defend herself—she was vulnerable and powerless to express disagreement or anger. Maybe this isn't completely divorced from the fear of castration, which is also about being rendered impotent. But in this case, you have to dig deeper and feel it through to understand the many layers of meaning. This is why no one can really tell you what your dreams mean. They can only get you started thinking about them.

More on Universal Meaning

In this book we'll cover standard, often correct, appraisals of certain dream symbols to help you see how interpretation works. It's a great way to start. But the real power is in your personal assessment of your symbols, especially those that might recur during your life and become the familiar, if not completely comprehensible, vocabulary of your dreams. With some practice, you'll be able to figure out what those personal symbols are and use them.

I have a couple of personal dream symbols, one of which portends troubled times ahead. I've had tornado dreams since I was a child. I see a beautiful, almost seductive, tornado in the distance, and I have to stand and watch it from a window. It comes close—sometimes it even passes through the space I'm standing in—but I'm never hurt. Freud would probably label it penis envy, but tornadoes are not symbolic of men in my personal dream code. I have concluded, from my own practice with dreams, that they stand for trouble ahead. (I suppose you could draw the conclusion that I see penises as symbols of trouble, but that feels a little contrived.) I witness the tornado's power, feel fear, but survive.

You'll find your own tornado, too. Dream symbols have a lot to do with your personal experience and predilections. In fact, your personal dream vocabulary is unconsciously chosen by you.

Alternative Theories on Dreams

Aside from our friends Freud and Jung, many other experts have weighed in with their own theories about dreams and what they are. Jane Roberts, author of *The Seth Material* and *Seth Speaks*, among other books, was a channeler who changed many minds about life and the world around us. In explorations of reality, karma, past lives, and spiritual paths, she channeled an entity called Seth. Seth's information was both fascinating and logical.

According to Seth, dreams are as real as waking life. Because of the way we sleep, our dream world is clearly divorced from our waking life. Dreaming is completely unreal to us, and according to Seth, our dream selves think that this waking life is one big joke, too. The gap can be closed, however, if you establish a different sleep pattern. Sleep no more than six hours at a time, suggests Seth, and get up and do some physical activity or go about your business for a few hours, then go back to sleep. Your physical body will benefit and you will be less separate from your dream self, enabling you to use your intuitive and telepathic powers in your daily waking life.

Seth proposes that what Freud and Jung call the "unconscious" is actually just your conscious self turned another way. Your conscious self literally leaves your body while sleeping, returning to check in once in a while.

If you have a desire to follow these instructions from Seth, read Jane Roberts's books (listed in Additional Reading) and try to alter your sleep habits. Those who have attempted it vouch for having heightened awareness and sharper consciousness.

Psychic Dreams

We all have dreams that can't be explained. These are what I call psychic dreams, concerning either prophecy, visitations from the dead, messages, or creative solutions to problems we can't solve in life. Since dreams defy categorization, you could have a dream that serves more than one purpose. Sometimes, though, dreams show up out of nowhere and don't make sense until a day or two later. My friend Danielle, a New Yorker, had this dream on September 10, 2001.

I am standing on the street corner across from my building looking up at my building. I am by myself; my family (kids, M——, and parents) are all inside the building. There is a traumatic happening affecting the building—I don't know what (fire? earthquake?). I am safe, but no one in the building is safe. I cannot go in the building, and no one can come out. I don't know what is happening inside the building.

Did Danielle's dream tell her something she could have acted on? No. Even if she knew it was a psychic/prophetic dream, could any action have prevented the terrorist attack? Not directly (see Chapter Seven for some ideas.) So why did Danielle's unconscious hook up with some weird dream realm? What purpose does that serve? Danielle's dream experience continued.

I've had this dream one more time since, the day before the blackout [on the East Coast in August 2003].

Oddly enough, both on September 11th and the day of the blackout, I found myself in a situation where every member of my immediate family was inside the building, and I was outside.

Danielle is very psychically sensitive, although she's more frightened of her gift than she is interested in developing it. Sometimes dreams will practically shout at you to show you your gifts, talents, and inner knowledge. Danielle had to reckon with the fact that she had a psychic experience. Now, if she wants to, she can learn how to use it.

Many people have dreams that whisper of momentous occasions. Dreams aren't just individual messages. Sometimes they're a broadcast code to tip off the world of what might be coming. Sometimes they provide you with touches of healing and access to higher understanding. Because these dreams can be so complex, you'll need to work up to understanding them. Build your dream experiences as you go through this book. You'll learn more details about psychic dreams when you're most practiced, in Chapter Six.

The Power of Positive Dreaming

You're probably aware of the power of positive thinking, in which a simple change of attitude or mindset can make things go your way. It happens with dreams, too. Although we all have our share of anxiety dreams and fear-related dreams, you also have dreams of being who you really want to be, of living the life you want. Your dreams can actually help you get there. You only have to be able to understand them and use them to make them work for you.

Getting to know your dreams is not as easy as it sounds. You'll remember some significant dreams, but you won't necessarily recall every dream (or even one dream) per night. You don't have to, but you do have to start training yourself to pay attention to dreams if you want to use them.

Once you recall a dream, you have to use both your intuition and your smarts to decide what it portends. Is it an indication of some future event? Is it a solution to a problem you're having at work? How do you know? With patience and practice, that's how. You'll become familiar with the kind of messages your dreams bring once you start to pay attention to them. It's hard to analyze your own dreams at first, but it gets easier with practice.

What you can do in your dreams will amaze you. Keep at it, and you'll see what I'm talking about.

WHAT'S AHEAD FOR YOUR DREAMS

- You have to start by remembering your dreams. This takes more practice than you might think.
- Once you're able to remember your dreams, begin to practice interpretation—decoding your personal dream vocabulary and interpreting the messages. It's not called practice for nothing!

- If you want to move on, ask your dreams to bring you answers. Still using interpretation, you can use your dreams in everyday life.
- Adventuring in dreams requires more skill. You can dream with lucidity and clarity—actually have your waking mind with you in your dreams.
- Dreams can ultimately bring your great spiritual fulfillment. You can use this creative, psychic realm to invoke peace and healing in your life and in the world around you.

ONE

Getting Started

Okay, you know how to sleep—at least I hope you do. But let's start at the beginning so you don't mess up your ability to dream from the word go.

First, forget falling asleep in front of the TV. Your dreams will incorporate the sounds from the television, the radio, traffic noises—any environmental sound—even though you're fast asleep. While you could still have vivid and telling dreams, you won't have a real insight into your personal dream symbols because the information coming in from outside will be clouding your unconscious. Learn to go to sleep without stimulus. I'm sure white noise is fine, but you might want to stay away from rain forest, ocean, or other nature sounds.

Dream Killers

TV
Noises throughout the night
Alcohol
Heavy meals
Super-spicy foods
Drugs (from cold medicine to marijuana—they're all bad for dreaming)
Waking up to an alarm

Second, for a few days, simply practice remembering your dreams.

You don't have to keep a dream journal, although it's obviously helpful to do so. In the beginning of dreaming to remember, try to wake up without an alarm and stay put in bed. You're going to be hazy in the first waking moments, and this helps in recalling dreams. You're most likely to remember the last dream of your night, typically the dream you have right before waking.

If you remember a dream, take time to describe it out loud or write it down, record it on your computer or onto a tape. All you're doing now is practicing remembering. You don't have to worry about interpretation.

Do this every day until you wake up and automatically remember to search your memory for your dreams. It takes time to train yourself. Be patient. I've been doing this for years and I don't remember every morning!

Once you've started to automatically remember that last dream of the night, stay in bed longer upon waking and change positions, rolling onto your other side to see if a dream comes back to you from that position. Some dream experts claim that your body position can help in recalling your dreams.

Remember, all you're trying to do is recall a dream. You don't have know what it means. The more skillful you are at remembering, the more you'll have to work with when you get into interpretation and exploration.

Get the Feeling

While we all struggle to remember the details of a dream, the real message of the dream is in the emotion. In the dream were you scared? Happy? Calm? When you woke up did you feel relieved? Did you get any feeling at all from your dream?

Since dreams are always symbolic, remembering detailed action and visuals only takes you so far. Say you dream of wrestling a giant squid. You might feel scared, overwhelmed, helpless, determined, or elated at conquering this problematic creature—the interpretation of this dream relies less on what a giant squid "means" than on what you feel about it.

It's extremely helpful to recite your dream out loud and in the present tense just after you wake up. Of course, it feels a little strange and, if you're not alone when you wake up, you might elicit some big-time teasing, but it really helps to ground your dream into your consciousness.

How to Remember and Ground Your Dreams

Let yourself wake up naturally, without an alarm.

Stay in your sleeping position in bed just after waking.

Give yourself time to think back to your last dream or most remembered dream of the night.

Recite your dream out loud, in the present tense.

Explore how the dream makes you feel; e.g., "I feel calm" or "I feel afraid."

Write down your dream in a place where you'll be able to find it again, such as a dream journal or diary.

Advanced Dreaming

Once you've got the hang of remembering a dream and grounding it in a journal, you could choose to take it a step further. Experts who have studied dreams for years keep their own dream journals and have trained themselves to record every dream, every night. You can do this, too, but you have to be pretty committed to the process—it takes a lot of time, and you have to get really good at deciphering your handwriting.

First, you have to train yourself to wake up after

every dream. You can do this by a simple suggestion before you go to sleep. Say to yourself, "Tonight, I wake up after each dream and I remember each dream." Always use the present tense—"I'm going to remember each dream" doesn't work as well. You have to make a statement. Not that I could tell you why, but that's how it works! This technique is the first step in a more advanced technique called "dream incubation," which we'll get to in Chapter Five, so don't gloss over it. Try it.

Talking to yourself before you go to sleep makes powerful and effective suggestions to your sleep-self. You can ask yourself to do anything you want in your sleep.

Second, make sure you have a pencil or pen near your bed as well as a notebook—large, if possible, so you can write your bleary-eyed, middle-of-the-night dreams down. You don't have to be fully alert or even put the light on to record a dream. In fact, I don't recommend it. With practice, you will learn how to write in the dark (or in a dimly lit room) and be able to decipher it in daylight.

We all have a different number of dreams per night—roughly every ninety minutes your body goes into REM sleep. But you won't be up all night writing. Even if you do wake up after a dream—and many of us do automatically—you may just roll over and go back to sleep. In the interest of full disclosure, I've never recorded more than two dreams per night.

Your interest level and commitment to your dream journal will have a lot to do with your success. You will dream every night, but how many you'll remember is up to your ability to ground them.

What's Your Excuse?

Ultimately, it doesn't matter how many dreams you have. It's only a matter of having enough so that you see a pattern in your dream symbols, learn to decode your dream messages, and have the ability to use your dreams to help you in your waking life.

In order to harvest enough dreams to learn your personal dream vocabulary, you'll have to commit yourself to this process. The upside of this task is that you go to sleep every night—it's not like you have to rework your schedule to suit a new exercise routine or change your diet. You're already set up to dream. But it will be up to you to remember them. Keep a log, and go back through it to see what your patterns are.

Don't be fooled by those easy-to-remember dream-dramas you already have in stock. Sure, those are relevant, even important, beginnings to your dream knowledge. Everyone has had colorful dreams that stick to memory files, but it's only the first layer. Recurring dreams, dramatic event dreams, even movie-star sex dreams are there to grab your attention. You're supposed to be curious about them; then you'll look further.

Start with the dreams you remember easily, and work at remembering more. You'll soon dig into some pretty amazing and bizarre levels of your own creative spirit.

TWO

Common Dreams: The First Layer

As you already know, you have a few dreams in mind that you remember. Chances are they're going to fall into one of the more common dream categories. This isn't to say that they're not important, but they're only the first layer. You remember these dreams because they grabbed your attention. It's a great place to start, but you'll get much deeper into more amazing dream space with a little practice.

Before you get into specific interpretation, let's look at some common types of dreams so you can familiarize yourself with reading between the lines (or is it between the sheets?).

Anxiety Dreams

Over time you'll find that your dreams come in different forms. When you're anxious, you'll get your personal brand of an anxiety dream. They can be dreams in which you feel intensely frustrated, weak, or without resources. These dreams can tell you something indirectly about your life.

> I have a recurring dream about wandering around an airport. When it comes time to board the plane I have to go through a maze of escalators, and I end up on what feels like an aircraft carrier (or a pier) in line. I never actually board the plane.
>
> —Janet, 26

You might think that you'd be better off without these dreams, but it's actually beneficial to express feelings of anxiety in sleep time, so that they don't necessarily have to come out during your waking life. You know that dreams are a different reality, but a connected reality. The work you do when you're dreaming, and it *is* work, can help you stay sane during the day. You'll never be able to fully rid yourself of unpleasant dreams, but you might grow to respect and read those dreams so you know what you're working through in daily life.

I had a weird dream last night about an ex-boyfriend. Just to give you a tiny bit of background, we dated for four years (in and after college) and had a very bad, prolonged breakup three years ago. I used to dream about him every night, but most of the time it would be dreams where we were together. Last night I had the most unusual dream about him—for some reason he was being honored in a big auditorium (like a lifetime achievement award, but I have no idea what it could be for), and his family and all sorts of friends were there, mostly people I didn't know. There were tons of people. I think he and I were together in the dream, and at some point I went to look for him. I walked in on him and another girl—and he tried to make all sorts of excuses, but it was completely obvious that they

> had been having sex. Anyway, I walked out and left, and it was the first time that I actually felt like, "What a scumbag. I don't need this." Then I woke up feeling pretty good about it. This may have to do with the fact that I had an amazing date with a new guy last week.
>
> —Penny, 28

At first Penny was annoyed that this guy invaded her dream space. But eventually it made sense to Penny that the dream she had about her last boyfriend was finishing up old business. She saw him get his "lifetime achievement award" and realized that he had achieved his purpose in *her* lifetime—she was free to get over him and be with someone else.

Nightmares

We all have them. It's part of the deal. Some people have terribly real, long, troubling nightmares. Some of us just have the run-of-the-mill horror shows that we can shrug off after a few hours. It's not always easy to figure out where nightmares come from—and they can be very disturbing if you're in a relatively happy place in your life. Keep in mind that nightmares are not omens. They are based on fears you'd rather deal with in the dream realm.

Gary had the following dream when he was having trouble at work. He was worried about a reorganization that would leave him without a job.

I am walking in my neighborhood. It is early evening. I realize no one is on the streets. It is too quiet. I feel a presence behind me—something I dread. I know I am in trouble. I run to the house closest to me—it's got a huge front porch and at first I can't find the door. Then I find it and I ring the doorbell. I pound on the door. I feel that something sinister is getting closer and it's going to get me. Finally the door opens—I don't know how. It's dark inside. This house isn't familiar. No one is there but I know I'm not safe. I feel a knife stab me. I try to scream but I can't. I try and try but I can't make a sound. I wake up.

—Gary, 38

Would Gary be stabbed in the back? His dream seemed to say so.

Nightmares can have a certain absurdity to them, which makes them easy to cast off as just a part of your imagination. It's a good thing, too, because if your nightmares were real, you might not survive them.

Some nightmares are just your unconscious mind exploring your fears or your dark side. Frankly, it's a lot better to do this in dream time than in real life. I once had a series of violent and frightening dreams in which I was beaten, stabbed, and chased. Although I had very little going on in my life to merit such unconscious circumstances, I assumed I felt persecuted and abused from something going on. Then I mentioned these dreams to my metaphysics teacher and she had an interesting take on it. Sometimes, she said, we choose to experiment with things in our dreams that we'd be horrified of in real life. I found it hard to believe, as you might, that anyone would choose to explore abuse or violence from either side—victim or bully—but on some level it did make sense. It's much safer to put yourself in grave danger in your dreams!

Death Is a Faker

Death appears in dreams for many people. In some cases, it's the dreamer who dies. In others, dreams are about a loved one dying. So the inevitable question: Is this prophetic?

No, not about somebody dying, anyway. Death is a symbol of change. Death in a dream typically is a message about change in your life.

Dreams about dying aren't about death at all.

When you wake up with your pillow soaking wet from nocturnal sobbing, you can be pretty sure that you're mourning a change in your life and not your own or someone else's death.

Real death—the impending death of someone in your life or someone who's already dead—doesn't come into your dreams as death. That is, if you're going to have a premonition about someone's death or if you're going to dream of someone who is dead, you can bet the dream won't be a sad one. You're more likely to get a message dream that is happy, peaceful, and calm. Frequently the person who is dying comes in a dream to let you know that he or she is okay.

A dream actually portending death is more often expressed as a journey or a trip. My friend Casey had a dream about her closest childhood friend, Marie, at the time Marie was suffering from a prolonged fatal illness.

I am in Paris with Marie, Connie [her mother] and Mike [her father]. They are staying at the Ritz Hotel. They are looking at carpets and they are going to buy Marie a carpet. It is beautiful—pinks and purples and flowers and angels—and it looks like a cross between a Chagall and a Warhol. There was a lot of running around and getting lost, and I kept coming back to the lobby of the hotel where they were looking at carpets. Marie was very tired.

—Casey, 38

Casey knew her dream was about Marie's death. Marie's parents had been dead for years, and here, in this beautiful hotel, a place of transience, they were selecting a carpet—in one interpretation, a magical carpet that can transport you anywhere—with flowers and angels on it. The colors, too, speak of a little girl (pink) and elevated/royal distinction (purple).

In her dream, Casey was trying to help, but she kept getting lost; she didn't know what to do or where to go. Marie's real-life situation was hopeless—there was no cure for her illness. Casey's dream made Marie's preparation for death beautiful and deliberate, just as Marie would have chosen for herself.

Here's another story. My friend Beth is well acquainted with the message of death in her dreams.

One I remember very well was a dream I had right before (like minutes before) my mother died. We were standing on a busy street corner and she turned to me, put an arm around me, and said, "Everything's going to be okay." I asked her if she meant she would recover, and she just smiled and said, "Everything's going to be okay."

I pressed her again and again for a more straightforward answer, and each time she patiently smiled and repeated that everything would be all right. The phone call that she had died was what woke me.

I've had subsequent dreams about my mother. Usually I begin them shopping or sitting at a kitchen table and chatting. As some point in the dream I turn to her and say, "But you're dead." Sometimes I cry at that point. She always looks at me and snaps (a bit pissed off), "If you're just going to cry about this, I'm not coming again!"

Remember—don't wig out if you dream about death. It's only change (which won't kill you).

Prophetic Dreams

It's hard to tell when a dream is prophetic, and usually you don't know it until an event confirms it.

I recently had a prophetic dream, but I didn't realize it until a few days later. It was just two days before I was to appear live on CBS's *The Early Show* to promote a book. I was excited, of course, to be on television, and the fact that the day of the broadcast was my birthday made it even more special. In my dream I was preparing to marry my husband. The room was set up; the flowers were in place. I was dressed and made up, but my husband didn't show up. Oddly, in my dream I was not furious (as I would have been in real life), but I was upset. I even remember thinking to myself, "I'm upset but I'm not freaking out—this is interesting." I knew that we would get married, but the wedding was simply delayed.

The night before I was to go on television, I got a call saying my appearance would be delayed. I would still go to the studio on my birthday, but my piece would be taped for broadcast at a later, still undetermined date. I was terribly disappointed and spent hours frantically e-mailing friends, family, and associates not to look for me on the show the next morning. My appearance was broadcast weeks later. I was out of the country, and most of my friends forgot to watch.

Was my dream a premonition of this disappointment? I think so. Did I know it at the time? No. More important, I don't think it would have mattered.

There isn't much you can do to brace yourself for a disappointment or even a death. Prophetic dreams are easy to spot in hindsight, after real life confirms the prophecy.

The Secret Dreams of Children

Your dreams as an adult are certainly more under your conscious control, but your childhood dreams were probably more open and psychically powerful. Children have less "editorial" faculties—they don't screen information the way we do as adults. They don't rationalize or laugh off dreams that seem uncomfortable or can't be explained. Here's an example of a dream that revealed a family secret.

> I haven't had this dream in more than twenty-five years, but I had it from my first memories until age seven or eight. I am walking down the stairway at my childhood home. I'm not sure why, but I need to get to the bright light at the end of the hallway (reachable by the stairway).

The ceiling is lined with big black spiders and the floor with fierce-looking crabs. As I try to make my way down the hallway, two little boys (probably eight or nine) are striking the crabs and spiders, clearing a path for me. One of the boys wears light blue pajamas, and I immediately recognize him as my older brother. The other boy wears red pajamas, and I don't know who he is (I assumed, as a child, he was a prince or my future husband).

When I was seven or eight a package arrived from my favorite uncle. It contained a note that read, "Dear Sandy [my mother], I thought you might want these," and a small stack of photographs featuring a boy in a red swimsuit running on the beach. I was thrilled because I recognized this boy as the boy from my dream. I took the stack and went to find my parents. I found my father first. He looked slowly at the pictures, shook his head, and said, "You're not supposed to see these. Your mother had a son who died, and these are pictures of your half brother, Stephen. Mommy didn't want to tell you until you were older." I never had the dream again.

It's worth noting that you can't hide information from the dream realm. Yet another reason to live life with integrity and truth!

Totally Real Dreams

If you've had a dream in which you actually wonder whether or not it's a dream—perhaps it feels really real, but it seems too weird to be real—you're on the verge of lucid dreams. It's not a world that is easy to get to and even harder to navigate, but most people happen into a dream like this once in a while.

Here's the thing about a lucid dream—it's *your* dream, so when you become lucid, instead of letting the action happen around you, you can control it. It's hard to imagine, but you can actually know that you're in a dream and direct the action just like it was a movie. You're the creator, not the supporting cast.

Some people get so into lucid dreams that they learn to wake themselves up in the dream and explore all sorts of new dimensions. This is clearly advanced dreaming and something we'll get to in Chapter Five.

For starters, though, it's easier to learn progressively, to practice remembering your dreams first, then move on to more sophisticated methods. You'll become more adept if you take it slowly, and you'll find that these interesting new layers of dreaming reveal themselves to you even before you've hit that part of the book. Your unconscious self is along for the ride, too, so you'll be getting to know a part of you that holds great creativity, strength, and humor. You'll get instant feedback in the dream world once you recognize this fascinating, powerful part of who you are.

Even without skill, your dreams connect you to the great spiritual realms of love and healing. You possess the power to use your dream life for creating the waking life you want. You will soon know how to use this power not only for yourself but to help the world. Really.

THREE

Interpretation, Part I: Simple Symbols and Dream Messages

There are many dictionaries of dream interpretation, some of them ancient texts and many written over the last twenty years. What they all have in common is the assumption that everyone shares the same symbols and that they all mean the same thing for each of us. This is the most dangerous fallacy of dream interpretation.

The first rule of dream interpretation is that there are no rules.

One person's good symbol is another person's most hated. For instance, cats in my dreams symbolize creative projects. But to my friend Liza, who hates cats, they are a symbol of something she dreads. Who's right? We both are.

Do not take any list of dream symbols as the gospel truth, not the suggestive lists in this chapter and certainly not the many dream dictionaries on the market. They are great jumping-off points for understanding your own dreams, but I urge you to use your intuition and sensitivity to feel how right those interpretations fit. One book may tell you that dreaming about watermelon is a symbol of giving birth or fertility, and another might say that it's about emotional issues. If neither one feels right, what do you do? You'll learn to go back into your dream and find out for yourself. It's that easy. (That watermelon could simply be a sign that you have to get up and pee—bursting with water, so to speak.)

I'm climbing some very steep stairs. The stairway is getting brighter as I go up. I sense there's light coming from the top, but I never get there.

I just keep climbing. But as I climb, I feel happier. I never get tired.

—Paloma, 29

At the time of this dream, Paloma was working on her dissertation. Whereas Freud might have viewed the stairs as phallic, she decided this dream meant she was getting close to the top, where there would be more light in her life. She figured her dissertation would soon be finished and that it would be successful. To her satisfaction, it was.

Speaking your dreams aloud will also reveal different levels of interpretation. The unconscious often sends us messages using puns and slang. Remember my friend who dreamed of mailboxes when she wanted to dream about guys? Mailboxes, male boxes. Dream about fighting with your boyfriend in a tent? Hmm, are things "intense"? How about someone insisting you buy Jimmy Choos (shoes) when in real life you've been wondering if you want to go out with a guy called James? Choos, choose. Oh yeah, puns are most definitely in your dreams.

Experts agree that dreams are a way for your unconscious to communicate with your conscious self. These are messages in your own dream code, and it's up to you to interpret them.

Once you have a dream that you remember pretty much from the beginning, through the middle, and to the end, you're ready for interpretation.

FIRST STEPS FOR INTERPRETATION

1. Describe the action of your dream in the present tense, out loud.
2. Report how you feel as the action is taking place.
3. Describe what you see, from something that just catches your eye to whether it's light or dark outside.
4. Describe the end and the feeling you have when you wake up.
5. Think it through: Any puns, slang, or people who stand for something else?

6. Feel it through: Is this feeling associated with something going on in your life right now?

I'm in an airplane. We're flying over a city, very close to the tops of buildings. I keep worrying that we're going to crash. The engines aren't on, and it's as if we're floating, not yet to safety, but we stay in the air. I'm sitting in business class, and I don't see anyone else around me, but I'm not alone. I wake up, worried, thinking of that airplane so close to crashing.

—Lilly, 27

This dream is clearly an anxiety dream, with the verb "worry" appearing twice. A plane is a vehicle, something that is supposed to take you somewhere—Lilly is on a journey that worries her. Lilly also mentions "business class," which is a clue. This dream is about the dreamer's work, not her social life or her family. She is worried about crashing, but somehow she's floating.

When I asked about this dream, Lilly agreed that

she was worried about her career, that she didn't know if she could do a job she'd recently been assigned, and that she was "getting away with it so far" but wasn't sure how it would turn out.

Without thinking and feeling it through, this dream could be interpreted simply on the surface—you wake up worried about a plane crashing. Yet if you take a few moments to go deeper, you could reveal a message to yourself and try to use it constructively. Lilly decided to get some input from her boss on her project and reduced her anxiety level significantly.

Examining your dreams helps you understand yourself, and the resulting sense of self-awareness increases you ability to make yourself happy.

DIY Dream Interpretation

Now that you're ready to practice looking at your dreams, let's get a few things straight.

First, don't believe the "facts" of your dreams. There are no facts. There are symbols. So you can stop tiring out your friends with your lengthy recitations of dreams in which you marry Prince William and asking them if they think it's going to happen. Sorry, you know the answer to that.

Second, just like that great dream when you marry a prince, those bad dreams don't come true either. Stop fretting every time you have a nightmare. Whatever your emotional state is during the day is probably being reflected at night. In other words, your nightmare is a result of some fear, anger, or conflict that already exists right under your nose (actually, right under your consciousness).

There are many ways to interpret dreams, and it is up to you to choose what works for you. Some dreams will be easy to understand through one method, while other dreams will make more sense another way. Dreams are malleable and come in many forms; you can't settle on only one formula. "One size fits all" doesn't apply to dreams!

Broad Interpretation

Since there are always layers to dreams, let's begin with the basic, broadest symbols and fundamental meanings. As you get into more specific details with your dream, you'll refine the dream message further. But start here, with elements, numbers, and colors, so that you have a strong foundation for decoding the message.

These broad clues correspond to humanity's interpretation of ancient symbols. Remember, you don't know that you know all of this—your unconscious mind is at work here. You innately retain a lot of wisdom, and it's from this well of internal knowledge that your dreams are born. It will take some time for you to get used to interpreting symbols. They aren't literal; they are only signposts to show you what you need to know or what you need to be addressing in your life. You'll probably find it completely natural—not at all weird—to begin to understand this ancient language.

Your unconscious self has a great deal of knowledge in storage. Jung thought of this information as a genetic code, a DNA for ancient wisdom passed down through the ages. Your ancestors gave you more than just your beautiful eyes.

Elemental Translations

One of my favorite ways to figure out the area in your life that is surfacing in your dream is to focus on the element most present in a dream. The four elements—fire, earth, air, and water—are the very stuff the world is made of, all that we need to survive.

Since the beginning of time as we know it, these elements have held sacred meaning, and each element represents a certain plane of life.

For instance, fire is the passionate, creative plane, so fire symbols—such as light, the sun, heat, and, of course, fire itself—might mean something going on in your working life. Fire is also a purifier, which makes it a symbol of change. Fire is sexy, but also dangerous.

Earth is the physical stuff, like buildings, your

body, and possessions. If you dream of gardens, a house, or "stuff" you might have, you're dreaming in the earth realm. Your dream is probably about your health, your physical self, or your financial situation.

Air is intellectual—thoughts and concepts. Air dreams, such as those in which you are flying through the air or there are notable winds, give you some insight into your mental state. Air can also be dirty, foggy, smoggy, or stuffy. Guess what that says about your mind? Not a lot of clarity there, maybe some confusion or misunderstanding. Dreaming that you are flying through supportive clear air or being held aloft by breezes is a way of showing yourself that you're in good mental shape—no reason to doubt your ideas or intelligence.

The element of water represents emotions. Rivers, lakes, oceans, swimming, rain, even baths, are giving you some insight into your emotional state. Floods are probably indicative of overwhelming emotions. Dry riverbeds? You feel that you have nothing to give, or that someone else has nothing to give to you. Swimming can mean that you are being supported by an emotional state, which is good. But if the water is murky, your emotional situation is unclear. If you dream that you're drowning, you're feeling overwhelmed and probably need to pause in your waking life to figure out what to do. Water occurs in almost everyone's dreams at one time or another.

Sometimes the elements of your dreams are pronounced—there's a fire, a storm, you're underwater or you're flying. If a dream has one or two dominant elements, you need to carefully consider what these messages mean. If no particular element stands out, you can move on to the next level of interpretation.

Element	*Sample Symbols*	*Interpretation*
Fire	heat, fire, sun	creativity, purifying
Earth	house, possessions	body, health
Air	wind, clouds, sky	mind, thoughts, ideas
Water	oceans, rain, rivers	emotions, feelings

Numbers

Are the numbers that come to you in dreams significant? Yes. Are they secret answers to the lottery? Very unlikely. Numbers, like elements, have ancient meanings that are stored in our unconscious minds. They're not that hard to understand. The number one, for instance, is solo, singular, alone. The number two is one with a partner—so that's about a twosome, a couple, a dual situation. There's actually a story, a life cycle, to numbers.

One stands alone.

•

One finds a partner and becomes two.

• •

They add to their family to make three.

• •
•

And then feel the need to grow further and get to four.

• •
• •

At four, they feel complete, steady, but a little inert. Five comes along and shakes up four—a problem that has to be faced.

• •
•
• •

To calm five down, another is added to make six.

• •
• •
• •

Six is a nice feeling, two sets of three. Again, there's a feeling of symmetry and roundness—and again, this strength and steadiness gives way to the desire to take a risk, so here comes one more, making it seven.

• •
• •
• •
•

The risk needs balancing again, and one more is added for the number eight.

• •
• •
• •
• •

Eight is a great achievement. Four pairs of twos, two sets of fours. Lots of accomplishment and steadiness. There is a celebration of this wholeness and one more comes into play. The last to join is the one who makes nine.

• • •

• • •

• • •

Here you have three sets of three, the triple trinity. There's nowhere to go from here but to start over—adding one to this makes ten, a one with a zero.

•

• •

• • •

• • • •

When you think about numbers and the stories they might tell, it's not so difficult to understand what they are doing in your dreams. You might dream of a number literally, or you might notice that there are two or three of something in your dream.

If you remember a number in whatever context it appears, it's probably meaningful.

My friend Anna once dreamed that she was the number 2. She literally became the number, and woke up in bed in the position (or at least trying to be in the position) of a number two. At the time, she was working hard on staying happy in a relationship. Forcing herself to be a number two in her dream was pretty telling—it wasn't an easy or natural fit, nor was her relationship, which eventually broke up. (It takes two, baby.)

Most of the time you'll dream of numbers in less literal ways.

> I had to get seven balls in the basket and one wouldn't go in. I tried and tried, but I couldn't do it. Finally my husband came and handed me the ball, and I made the basket.
>
> —Ling, 34

In this dream, my client recalled how she found herself on a basketball court and she needed to make seven baskets. That last one only worked with the help of her husband. In her life, she was trying to make a change in her job. The basketball court; where you score points and "win," was her dream code for work. The number seven is a symbol of change. Her dream was about letting her husband help her make the change she wanted.

Numbers, like elements, appear in your dreams in varying ways. Maybe you'll remember that you were wearing two bracelets or that there were five rooms in your house. There are plenty of ways for numbers to find their way into a dream. But it's up to you to decode what they mean in your life.

Even if a number is gigantic, you can try out its meaning. The way to do this is to reduce it numerologically. As an example, take the number 45,938. If you happen to remember this or any other large number from a dream, add each individual number up until you get to a single digit: 4 + 5 + 9 + 3 + 8 = 29; 2 + 9 = 11; 1 + 1 = 2. The number 45,938 is actually the number two, in a more complicated disguise. I know it's hard to believe that your unconscious could go to all that trouble to say "two," but it can.

Chances are, you won't remember a huge number

like that from your dream. But, say you dream of a shorter number, such as fifty-seven or ninety-nine. You can interpret those numbers in two ways. First, look at each number separately.

The number fifty-seven is composed of a five and a seven, so you can look at the meaning of those numbers individually. You can also add up the digits—5 + 7 = 12; 1 + 2 = 3—and look up the number three as well.

For ninety-nine, consider the two nines—and see what double meaning the number nine might have for you. Then reduce the number: 9 + 9 = 18; 1 + 8 = 9. You'll see that it's about nine again. Dreams can be very insistent!

Below are the basic interpretation of numbers. Remember, you can play the lotto if you want, but the real reward is learning what your unconscious is trying to tell you.

Number	*Meaning*
1	solo, being alone, initiation
2	partnership, couples, balance
3	growth, positive energy, the trinity

Number	*Meaning*
4	equilibrium, balance, stasis
5	conflict, discomfort, a creative state
6	harmony, prosperity, happiness
7	risk, change, exploration
8	rewards, satisfaction
9	the ending, "three threes," closure

Take your time to interpret numbers in your dreams. Don't force a meaning when it doesn't feel right, and remember that the numbers appear in the context of a dream, so you have to look at all the symbols surrounding it as well as how you felt in your dream. Numbers are guides. They function in support of the all the other stuff in your dream (unless you dream that you actually *are* a number, as did my friend Anna, but that's not something you'll encounter very often).

Ancient Numbers and Archetypes

One step deeper into the interpretation of numbers and symbols leads to the world of tarot and very old, unconscious associations with archetypes of the soul's journey. If you happen to dream about a number between zero and twenty-one, be sure to check out both the classic numerological interpretation (see list on pages 65–66) and the following ancient meaning. You'll know in your gut when you've hit the right chord.

You've probably heard of tarot cards. The use of tarot cards is an ancient form of divination based on classic archetypes of life. Archetypes are simply images or models of a stage of life—the fool, for instance, is the beginner. You're the fool when you first decide to go into the world on your own, getting your first apartment or your first job. The fool visits us at different stages in our lives, whenever something new is about to open up. The fool is associated with zero. If you do dream of the number zero, don't immediately interpret it as a message of null or nothing. It just might be the fool showing up to tell you you're ready for something new!

Some of the archetypes below are going to sound strange. Don't take them literally. It's not as if you're going to be "Death" or that you'll suddenly have an audience with the "Pope." These are only symbolic names.

Major Arcana

Number	*Traditional Tarot Name*	*Modern Interpretation*
0	Fool	Potential
1	Magician	Entrepreneur
2	Virgin	Intuition
3	Empress	Feminine power
4	Emperor	Masculine power
5	Pope	Hierarchy
6	Lovers	Partnership
7	Chariot	Victory
8	Strength	Strength
9	Hermit	Introspection

Number	Traditional Tarot Name	Modern Interpretation
10	Wheel of Fortune	Fate
11	Justice	Justice
12	Hanged Man	Surrender
13	Death	Transformation
14	Temperance	Patience
15	Devil	Expediency
16	Tower	Disruption
17	Star	Hope
18	Moon	Hidden elements
19	Sun	Vitality
20	Judgment	Forgiveness
21	The World	Totality

Colors

People often ask me if everyone dreams in color, or if there are those who dream in black and white.

Most experts contend that you dream in both and that you actually dream in whatever colors you want. If dreams are symbolic messages, why wouldn't the color you dream in tell you something, too?

Of course, if you dream in regular, everyday color, you don't have to get into heavy color interpretation. It's not really worth it, since your dream is putting conventional life, or your expectation of normal life, into your dream. It's not a message in itself.

Color becomes more symbolic when one or two colors become dominant in your dream, you see colors changing in some way, or you simply vividly remember a color as a significant detail of your dream. Don't worry about remembering the color of every little thing from your dreams. Just interpret colors you clearly remember since they are probably significant.

It is summer, early evening, beautiful with a soft summer breeze but not the usual steamy St. Louis sludge. An idyllic evening. I have music on. It feels like a night in high school when anything is possible, when everything is full of potential. I am getting dressed and I hear Wyn coming, and I run to the window to watch him approach the door. I know he is dead, but I am not surprised to see him. He is blue from head to toe (instead of his usual soft brown), and his hair is a little longer (it was kept compulsively cropped close to his head) and blue, too, and I think, "Oh, I guess all the cool ghosts are blue," because Wyn was always very distinctive in his style and very, very cool. I hear the familiar creaking on the stairs, but at the same time he kind of comes through the window. I am so excited and thrilled and tingling to see him. I hold on to him and want him to stay, but he says he is just stopping by. I say, "But let's go eat, let's go to . . ." (and I list all these things we liked to do), and he says no, he has to go, but he is holding on and touching my hair (we were always very physically affectionate). I get irritated and say, "You can see all those other ghosts all the time. I don't even live in this house anymore, and you are all blue." I keep bringing up the blue thing; maybe that irritated him. "You never come to New York. Please stay." And he still ends up floating away. But I was still really grateful in the dream and also when I woke up.

—Joelle, 32

Clearly, the color blue figured prominently in Joelle's dream. She wasn't sure if this dream was a visitation from her dear dead friend or just a fantasy, until we looked at it together.

In Joelle's dream, her best friend, who died many years before, visits her from the spirit plane. Blue is the color of ascension, of spirit and purity, and Joelle took this to mean that her dream had been real; this was clearly Wyn visiting her as a spirit. Her dream space melded with the spirit world where she could feel "at home." (While Joelle has wanted to be able to dream of Wyn again, he's never made another appearance—at least that she remembers.)

Colors can be interpreted in a number of ways when they appear in your dreams, so again, use the meanings that make the most sense to you. How you were brought up has a profound effect on the meaning of certain colors, too. For the Chinese, fiery red is a positive, lucky color, while to Westerners it's a stop sign and a sign of anger, like the red flag waved at a bull. It's best if you can remember how you reacted to a color in your dream or if it made any impression on you at all. Colors are part of the message, not the message itself. Here are some generalities to keep in mind:

Red arouses passion or anger. It basically grounds you so that you are alert and in a state of readiness. It's a color of energy, blood, life source, and power.

Pink is a color associated with little girls and romantic idealism. If there is an obvious pink tinge to your dreams, consider what part of your life is still influenced by your hopeful, idealistic youth.

Orange is a color that brings out emotional responses. Orange can portend success (like gold the color or the metal). It's a color associated with harmony, pride, ambition, and strength.

Yellow represents the sun and vitality, brightness and purification. But yellow has another side—it can mean cowardice as well.

Green is a color of life and abundance (which is why our money is green). That's the positive side. Green also means mold and slime—so make sure you have a sense of how that green in your dream made you feel.

Blue is a spiritual color. It's pure, clear, and calm. Blue in dreams can be a sign of an important spiritual message. The Virgin Mary's color is blue, another association with spiritual or religious significance. Look carefully, though; blue can also mean depression, as in "having the blues."

Purple is a royal color. Generally, it's a good dream color because it indicates dominance or success for you. However, too much of a good thing can lead to pomposity or excess.

Brown represents earthiness and stability. Brown is also the color of excrement, which can mean abundance (the good) and filth (the bad).

Gray is a middle tone. Since it rests between black and white, what you've got here is a transition, neither good nor bad.

White is a spiritual and ritualistic color associated with purity. Strong white color in your dreams would most likely give you a feeling of open space and possibility, the infinity of spirit. It can also mean blankness, which is the same thing, only somewhat negative.

Black is the color of mystery. It's the unknown, the unconscious. Black is a sacred color and can indicate the gestation of a new part of you. Black also represents your fears, mourning, or destruction.

FOUR

Interpretation, Part II: It's in the Details

So far we have considered elements, numbers, and colors. They all bring a new dimension to the way you look at your dreams, broad messages you might not have been aware of. Yet we haven't even arrived at the obvious symbols—the people, things, and situations that appear in your dreams. What about that creepy taxi driver who won't take you where you want to go, or that hot night with Russell Crowe that didn't go on long enough? You'll wake up thinking one thing about your dream, but when you're done interpreting you'll have a whole new understanding.

People

First, most therapists will tell you that every person in your dream is a symbol of you. Even if you dream of your sister, it's not really about your sister but what she stands for in your life. Same goes for boyfriends, bosses, teachers, monsters, mothers, kids, and yep, Russell, too. The people in your dreams are all a reflection of some part of you or the personification of some emotion. Even in prophetic dreams, there's always a layer of symbolism to the people or situations you see.

I can't get to my then-boyfriend. I can see him, but he's on the other side of a glass wall, or I'm trying to call, but I can't remember his phone number or some such. We're not together anymore (surprise, surprise, he wasn't emotionally available, and the relationship ended).

—Virginia, 27

To begin understanding the people in your dream, disregard their identity and try thinking of them as a "type" or character. For instance, if you dream you have a fight with your boss, ask yourself how you feel about authority figures in your life. Is this a likable authority or someone you don't respect? If you dream of a boyfriend who leaves you, is this a guy whom you loved and who treated you well or someone who wasn't really good for you? What were his shortcomings? Virginia had her dream when she was dating someone new. This relationship also didn't last because he was emotionally distant. Her dream was telling her that the same thing was happening.

Your dream people are bringing you messages about your current world. Whether it's hidden hostility, lost love, or current relationship problems, your dreams will pull in people who symbolize the action. This is to help bring unconscious messages to the surface so that issues may be addressed.

I had a dream last night that I was literally climbing my way out of a deep ditch. Although it was strange, I don't think I was frightened. I

> was also talking to my sister who was cheering me on and helping me get out of the ditch. In my dream I was concerned about what neighborhood I was in, that there were some Orthodox Jews in part of the neighborhood and maybe that would be a problem—although, in the dream, I was thinking it wouldn't be so bad.
>
> —Joan, 32

In Joan's dream, her sister is cheering her on to get out of a ditch. In her life, Joan was working on getting out of debt (the ditch), but her freelance work wasn't bringing in enough money. In her dream, she thinks there are Orthodox Jews in her neighborhood but that it's not a problem. How does that relate? To Joan, Orthodox Jews represent a confined society, a rigid structure of rules that controls what women do. Joan took some time to figure out how that related to her own life, then settled on the fact she was afraid that a full-time job at a company would restrict her ability to feel creative and free, and that she'd be controlled by authority, or in her terms, a bunch of men. Orthodox Jews were a symbol of men in the business world, but in her dream they didn't make her feel restricted from getting out of her hole. She realized that her dream was telling her to keep going, not to be afraid of taking a job—that even if there is a rigid structure of authority, it won't bother her.

The people you dream about are rarely the real stars of your dream. Look into what they stand for in your life to find what they mean in your dreams.

It's hard not to interpret dreams literally when you dream about someone who is close to you. A mother who dreams of leaving her baby on a train feels guilty and horrified all day, even though the dream had nothing to do with her actual children. Dreams can be highly charged with emotion and can cast a shadow over your day if you don't take time to figure out what they're trying to tell you. Here's a doozy I had just after giving birth to my daughter.

I was riding on a train with my newborn twins. They were wrapped in blankets and outside it was horribly cold and snowy. We were traveling in the countryside, something like the Russian winter in *Doctor Zhivago*. The train stopped just before a tunnel. I got off the train with my babies and started to walk in the snow. I knew that I couldn't take my babies with me. I buried them in a snowbank and left, going somewhere I needed to be (I don't know where). At the time I felt fine, thinking that the babies would preserve well in the cold. Suddenly I thought, "I'm a mother! I can't leave babies in the snow—they'll die!" and I woke up, so upset I cried.

My baby daughter was fast asleep in her crib, but I was distraught. After I calmed down I took a few minutes to think about the dream. It wasn't easy to remember those images—the cold, the train, leaving my babies in the snowbank. It was very upsetting. I applied this exercise to keep myself from falling apart again:

What was the main theme of the dream?

I was trying to get somewhere and the babies weren't as important as where I was going.

Who were the main characters?

My babies and I.

Who or what could they stand for?

This took some consideration, then I realized that babies can be interpreted as creative projects. I had two books lurking on the back burner, about to be published. I realized that these were probably the twins. Two books, two creative projects, two babies.

How did I feel about the characters?

I was anxious about the two babies, but I didn't have a problem abandoning them to get where I needed to go. In the dream, for a while at least, I felt they would "keep."

How does this apply to what they stand for?

At the time, I was absorbed in motherhood. I was much less worried about launching my books than I would have been before giving birth to my daughter. I was willing to let go of the books, let them "keep" until I was ready and able to deal with them.

At the time, this dream made sense just as I explained above. In retrospect, I realize that the train was my "journey" into motherhood and that winter reflected how harsh and difficult those first few months were. Because that dream was so profound, it has stuck in my consciousness, still as fresh as it was the night I dreamed it. But it doesn't freak me out anymore. Those two books found their way into the world slowly and without much guidance from me. The "twins" were just fine, and it was the right thing to do, to leave them in the snow.

Ask yourself a number of questions as you try to understand the nature of your dream characters. A mischievous little boy in your dream might remind you of kids who got away with something in your past, so he might be a symbol of deceit. A quiet, dark stranger might at first make you fearful, but then you realize this person doesn't do anything to cause you harm. Is this a representation of your shadow, your mystery? It's quite possible. Your grandmother might represent your ancestry or female wisdom. Russell

Crowe (or whoever might captivate you in your dreams) could be about pleasure and allowing yourself to let go. Famous people in dreams are probably simply the representations of the qualities you see in them.

Questions to Ask Yourself About Your Dream Characters

Who are the main characters in the dream?

What could they stand for?

How does this situation feel compared to what is going on in your life?

How old is this person?

- Young could mean something new or from your youth
- Old could be experience or wisdom, or something dying

How does this person's gender make you feel?

What does the race of this person represent?

Attitude: Is this a person who is helpful, scary, wise?

The Face of Fear

So many dreams address our fears—many of them through scary characters. Whether we consciously feel fear or we suppress it, it surfaces so easily at night. Have you ever considered who embodies your fears?

Do you see a famous bad guy, or is there someone from your life who represents fear in your dreams? Is it a faceless, lurking presence or someone you can identify? It's important and extremely useful to understand your personal fear symbols. You'll be much more conscious of your fears in waking life and, consequently, address them more effectively.

Try to establish a list of characters who show up in your scary dreams. Not only will you enjoy deciphering the symbolism, which can actually be amusing, but you'll be able to release your fears with greater understanding.

Remember, people in your dreams aren't really personal. They are symbols, messages and messengers that take time to decipher. Is it a menacing grandmother? A crying baby? Your first impulse is to take that person literally, but if you pick apart the composition of the character, you'll see it very differently.

The Language of Animals

Animals, too, bring significant dream messages. A spider with teeth, for example, is a pretty good symbol of something ominous. A dog, though, is a nice symbol of loyalty and friendship. If you do dream of an animal, consider what quality it may represent. You can use the following chart as a guide, but please make sure that the meanings assigned to each animal feel right to you. These are your animals, your symbols. While birds frequently mean imagination, to you they might be terrifying creatures; in that case, birds in your dreams represent fear.

Typically, when I'm overwhelmed, rodents, in large numbers, find their way into my dreams.

—Fran, 22

Also, look at how the animal acts in your dream. Is it friendly? Threatening? Does it notice you, or does it remain outside of the action? Describing the context of the dream is important in deciphering what the animal is trying to tell you or what it represents.

Common Interpretations of Animals

Animal	*Interpretation*
Ant	Hard work
Bear	Resurrection, strength, fortitude
Bee	Immortality, order, work
Bird	Transcendence, imagination
Buffalo	Supernatural power, strength
Butterfly	Immortality, transformation
Cat	Mystical wisdom
Deer	Swiftness

Dog	Loyalty
Dolphin	Worldwide guide, safety, swiftness
Dove	Life spirit, soul, peace
Duck	Superficiality
Eagle	Sky gods, the sun, victory
Elephant	Strength, fidelity, memory
Elk/Moose	Supernatural power
Falcon	Victory
Fish	Purification, spirituality
Fly	Evil
Fox	Slyness
Frog	Fertility, eroticism
Gazelle	Spirit, liberation
Goat	Superiority
Goose	Longevity
Grasshopper	Carelessness
Hawk	Royalty, nobility

Hen	Fertility
Heron/Stork/Crane	Vigilance, quietness
Horse	Swiftness, reason
Lamb	Innocence, youth
Lizard	Silence
Mouse	Agitation
Otter	Cleanness, playfulness
Ox	Patience, toil
Parrot	Imitation
Peacock	Immortality, vanity
Pig	Fertility, greed
Ram	Virility
Raven	Prophecy

I'm standing on a street in New York City somewhere in Midtown where there are lots of tall office buildings. It's daytime and there's the usual traffic and pedestrians. Nothing seems out of the ordinary. Suddenly a big bee, the size of a fist, flies over my head and I'm scared. It doesn't menace me, but it won't go away. I put out my hand to shoo it away, and it sort of grips my hand, leading me somewhere. My arm is extended upward, the bee is attached to me, and I'm walking swiftly to keep up the pace. I keep waiting for it to sting me, but it doesn't. I wake up.

—Sarah, 32

Sarah didn't immediately understand this dream when she shared it with me. In her dream she was afraid of the bee, but as it attached itself to her, she was more fascinated by its size and strength. She allowed the bee to lead her somewhere, some place still unknown, but the fear was gone.

With a little thought, Sarah decided that the dream was telling her that she could gain speed and recognition in her career if she worked hard. Since Sarah had been toying with changing her career path, she took the dream to mean "stick with it," interpreting the big bee as a symbol of hard work and strength.

Piling on the Symbols

Most dreams have more than one layer. We've covered elements, colors, numbers, people, and animals, but we can go even deeper. Where was your dream? What was the action in the dream? Was this a recurring or a common dream? If so, what does that mean to you?

The following pages give you further fuel for dream interpretation, although these lists aren't the last word on what your dreams mean. To get to know more about your dreams, simply use these symbols as a jumping-off point. If what you dreamed about isn't here, try to decipher what it represents in your life. It's vital that you establish your own dream language, because dreams are personal messages to you. That said, here are a few ways of looking at more dream symbols.

Common Dream Places

Place	*Interpretation*
House or building	Your life or body
Hospital	A situation that needs mending
Hotel	A place of transition
Prison	Restriction
Office	Hard work, solving a problem
School	Learning about something new
Dark room	No answers yet
Messy room	Problems
Dilapidated room	Something needs your attention
Car	You, where you're headed
Road	Your life
Dirty bathroom	Dealing with other people's crap

Common Dream Action

Action	*Interpretation*
Going upward	Dealing with the outer world
Going down	Dealing with internal issues
Opening a door or window	Opening to a new experience
Not going through a door	Not facing a problem
Dying	Changing, starting afresh
Having a baby	Starting a new project
Losing a baby	Your project may not be viable
Being naked	Vulnerability
Making love	Wanting to connect
Losing teeth	Self-esteem issues, unexpressed anger
Flying	Freedom, feeling good

Action	*Interpretation*
Falling	Fear, losing control
Being pursued	Anxiety

I'm in a dark room. It doesn't feel scary, but I can't find my way around. I'm walking carefully because I feel I might step on something. I put my arms out and tentatively reach for something to hang on to. I'm getting more nervous now, although not afraid for my life. I'm more afraid of making a mistake. I feel a table next to me. There's a lamp on it. I feel the switch at its base and turn it on. The light is soft, and the room is now visible. It's beautiful! Lovely old books, comfortable chairs, a hearth. I'm going to make a fire. Then I wake up.

—Terri, 32

Terri had this dream just before making a decision about going back to school for a law degree. According to classic dream symbolism, Terri was afraid of taking the wrong step in the dark room (her situation). The lamp illuminated the room filled with books (knowledge) and chairs (places to feel at ease) and a hearth where she was going to light a fire before she woke up. Back to the elemental symbols, the fire she wanted to light represents her passion, her work energy and purification.

Not all dreams incorporate such complete and obvious imagery. In fact, most of your dreams are going to be a lot weirder than this one. Use your heart and gut instincts before you use your mind for interpretation. The laws of logic are rarely respected in dreams.

General Symbols

Symbol	*Interpretation*
Acorn	Life
Anchor	Steadfastness

Symbol	*Interpretation*
Apple	Wisdom, fertility, love, forbidden fruit
Arrow	Power, phallus
Balances	Justice, impartiality
Bones	Life structure
Book	Wisdom
Bow	Willpower
Bowl	Feminine power, vagina
Box	Womb
Candle	Light in darkness, illumination
Chalice	Inexhaustible abundance
Circle	Totality
Compass	Unerring, impartial justice
Cornucopia	Abundance
Crowd of people	The need to make a decision
Crown	Victory, dignity, honor

Symbol	*Interpretation*
Crystal	Purity, knowledge
Cube	Stability, completion
Dice	Fate, fickleness
Earth	Nourishment
East	Dawn, hope, youth
Egg	Life structure, creation
Elm	Dignity
Evergreens	Immortality, vitality
Eye	Omniscience, intuitive vision
Gargoyle	The ability to scare away evil
Fan	Spirit, dignity
Feather	Truth, lightness, air
Feces (your own)	Making money, abundance
Feces (someone else's)	Other people's crap
Feet	Movement
Fir tree	Boldness, integrity

Symbol	*Interpretation*
Flame	Purification, transformation
Flowers	Opened potential
Forest	Realm of the psyche
Fountain	Eternal life
Fruit	Immortality, fertility
Garden	Paradise, abundance
Gate	Entry, communication
Globe	Eternity, universe
Glove	Honor
Gold	Illumination, wealth
Grain	Potentiality
Grapes	Wisdom
Grass	Submission, usefulness
Gun	Phallus
Hammer	Masculine force
Hat	Authority

Symbol	*Interpretation*
Helmet	Protection, preservation
Horn	Supernatural power, divinity
Horseshoe	Good luck
Hourglass	Cycle of life and death
Iron	Strength, inflexibility
Ivy	Immortality
Jewels	Hidden knowledge, something precious
Knife	Sacrifice, phallus
Ladder	Passing from one place to another
Lake	Magic
Lamp	Wisdom
Lemon	Sharpness
Mill	Fate
Mirror	Truth, self-realization

Symbol	*Interpretation*
Moon	Feminine power, mystery
Mountain	Constancy
Net	Ensnaring, entanglement
Oak	Strength, courage
Oar	Power, skill
Obelisk	Phallus, male power
Orchid	Magnificence
Palm	Righteousness, fame
Pillar	Connection of heaven and earth
Pine	Uprightness, vitality
Pinecone	Good fortune
Plants	Life force
Rainbow	Different states of consciousness
Salt	Incorruptibility
Sand	Impermanence
Seed	Latent power, potentiality

Symbol	*Interpretation*
Shells	Feminine, life, birth, regeneration
Shield	Protection
Ship	Safety
Smoke/Steam	Confusion about anger
Spear	Masculine force, phallus
Sphere	Perfection
Square	The physical aspect of earth
Star	Divinity
Stone	Stability, durability, reliability
Sword	Protection, authority, phallus
Teeth	Sex, anger, self-esteem
Tornado	Unpreventable, brief threat
Triangle	Heaven, the planet Earth, man (or father), mother, child
Volcano	Anger
Wallet	Identity

A woman I know had this dream years ago, but it still sticks with her because it was so bizarre. She was pregnant when she had the dream:

I dreamed that President Clinton was chasing me and wanted to shoot me dead.

—Betsey, 44

If you analyzed Betsey's dream for her, where would you start? First, you know that she's pregnant in real life; a big change (a new baby) is coming soon. Being chased is a common dream theme, sometimes indicating feeling threatened or under pressure. Now, what about President Clinton? He's trying to kill her, to "shoot her dead." If you go back to the symbols we've covered, you'll see that death represents change, so the president is chasing her to change her. And a gun, going all the way back to Freud, is a symbol of a penis. The libidinous former president certainly makes a good dream symbol for sexual contact. Crude as it sounds, this dream was a simple argument from Betsey's unconscious that her pregnancy (caused by a man) was going to change her life, and she was feeling the pressure.

Consider how it feels to be pregnant. You're excited about a baby coming, but you see your body morphing into very strange shapes and states. You look forward to being a mother, but you're also scared of the unknown. A new baby, whether it's your first or third, is going to throw your life into chaos for a while. Looking at this dream from a symbolic perspective, it's a perfectly normal, perfectly respectable way of expressing anxiety without having it surface in daily life. This dream stuck in Betsey's mind because it seemed strange, but, after reflection, it's not weird at all.

More on Symbols

It's not just the thing you see in your dream; it's how you react to it. Here's where your part comes in. When you go through your dreams and note each symbol, recall how you felt about it. Let's say you love chocolate pudding (and I, for one, do); a big serving of chocolate pudding in your dream might be a symbol of goodness, or perhaps something you feel is a sweet indulgence or a treat. But what if that pudding made you feel sick in your dream? It may be a sign that someone or something you like isn't good for you. The way you react to what you dream is key to understanding its meaning.

Sally studied her dreams for years by herself and with a psychotherapist. The dream below is one that she has harbored since her childhood, and her personal interpretation (with the help of a professional) follows.

For years as a child I had a recurrent nightmare that I was rolling down a hill—a very particular hill near my home. In my dream this was a much steeper hill than it really is, and my head was going to smash into a black lamppost at the bottom of the hill. I'd awake with a jolt, sweating. Now, as an adult, I have become enough of a Freudian to interpret this one!

I see the dream as an anxiety dream about my relationship with my father, whom I adored and who terrified me when he was drunk, which was often. I wanted love from him and got a mix of inappropriate fondling and expressions of his

> private anguish and sadness. So I see the dream as partly fear of my out-of-control father, and of being out of control in my feelings for him, sexually, and imagining him as a phallic shape that could hurt me.

Dream Dissection

Dreams such as the one Sally had above have many layers to them. Sally wouldn't have arrived at such a specific interpretation for her dream on her own. But not all dreams demand the attention of a professional interpreter, and your instincts can help you find the pertinent meaning of a dream. You can always ask a friend to help you.

Regina and I decided to dissect the following dream together, step by step, the way you could do it on your own. Read the dream, then follow along as we prod, poke, and push our way through dream symbols.

> I was standing in front of a store window. It was totally bright and gorgeous, filled with designer

bags and jeans and all this jewelry. I'm standing there, thinking I want to go in. I don't move, though. I feel something happening. Suddenly this really scary guy comes running out of the store screaming, "It's crashing, it's crashing!" I don't know what he means—the stock market?—but I get the feeling something bad has happened. I walk away fast, looking over my shoulder to make sure no one is following me.

—Regina, 26

What do the handbags, jeans, and jewelry mean to you?
I wanted that stuff. I love it all. I wish there was really a store like that.

How did that bright light make you feel?
I wanted to go in there, like it was going to make me happy.

How did you feel standing there, at the window?
I felt outside of things. I felt like I could go in the store but that I was a little afraid. I don't know, a little shaky on what I should do.

How did you feel when the screaming man came out?
I was startled and then kind of scared. He wasn't talking to me, but I never would have expected this guy to come out of a store like that.

What does "it's crashing" mean in your life?
I don't know. The stock market? Maybe crashing waves? Crashing on someone's couch?

If something crashes, what happens to it?
It falls apart.

And how does a guy like this make you feel?
He's someone I would stay away from. A crazy man. I don't get involved.

So let's put this together. You're in a situation where you really want something that you think is going to make you happy. Then a guy runs out warning everyone that something is crashing, and you avoid going into the store. What's going on in your life?
I'm looking for a job. There's a job I really want at a biotech company that does stuff with

DNA. But everyone is telling me that it's not a good job because biotech companies fail so often.

Interesting. You're looking at something you want, like in this store window. You want to go in, but a guy tells "everyone" that something's crashing and you walk away. What was in the window again?
Jewelry, jeans . . .

Jeans. Ever think about that word?
Jeans. Genes! Oh, my God—like in DNA.

Now tell me how you felt when you woke up.
I felt safe. But I still want to go back to that store.

What do you think that tells you?
I want that job.

That would be my guess, too.

I took Regina back into her dream by having her close her eyes, visualize the dream, and narrate it up to the point the guy runs out screaming. Then, instead of walking away, I asked her to go into the store and see what was happening.

I walk in and there are people shopping, trying on clothes, and I just go in to look around. There's nothing crashing. It's a cool place.

Regina decided to go for the job at the biotech company despite the opinion of other people.

Going Back into a Dream

Yes, it's possible to go back into a dream, but I don't mean by going back to sleep. If certain dreams leave you with an unfinished feeling as did Regina's dream, you can go back into a dream and do something differently. Find out what would happen if you said yes instead of no. This isn't dreaming—it's more like self-hypnosis.

This is easiest done with someone else who can act as the interrogator as you revisit the dream. Having someone to talk to and help you through the dream can leave you more open to seeing what's there. It really works, especially with dreams that feel unfinished, those dreams you keep thinking about.

Revisiting a Dream: An Exercise

Find a place where you can relax. Turn off any phones or other distractions. Close your eyes. Speak your dream out loud from the beginning. Include as much detail as you can, allowing yourself to feel immersed in the dream. When you get to the part where the dream ended originally, continue the action. It's important to note exactly how you feel at this point. The emotion or gut feeling you have as you continue the action will release the dream's impression and give you the information you need to feel complete.

As I was writing this book I had this dream:

I'm standing in a large oval-shaped restaurant. The tables are crowded with people enjoying themselves. There is lots of blue, too. There seems to be an ice-skating rink in the middle of this restaurant, but there's no ice in it. I think I see a woman I used to work with (who was my mentor for a time) sitting at a table against the rim of the rink. I'm pretty sure it's her, and I walk into the empty rink and approach her. She sees me and recognizes me, too, but doesn't seem surprised. It's been about seventeen years since I've seen her. We talk. Her teenage daughter is there, too.

I wake up, feeling the dream is incomplete. I want to know what the blue means, what the oval means, why I saw this woman in my dream. I go back into the dream and I feel it right away.

This time I ask Sharon, my old friend, if I can sit down with her, and we talk about the old days in advertising. We laugh and things feel very comfortable. She tells her daughter that I'm cool.

I emerged from this second dream visit and felt complete. It was an acknowledgment. My mentor had acknowledged that I was successful now on my own. As a result of that dream, I got back in touch with her. It was a nice push to reconnect with a special influence in my life. And it gave me a little pat on the back for the feast (the restaurant) my life is now.

A Word on Words

Another layer that should be examined lies in the words associated with your dream. Dreams are symbolic in funny ways—not just in the things, colors, and numbers that might come up in a dream but the actual words you use to describe your dream.

Regina talked about "jeans" when her subconscious meant "genes." It's not easy to decode your dream when you're only looking at what's *in* it, rather than what it *sounds* like.

Slang, too, loves to show up in dreams. Can you imagine how many ways you can use slang phrases in your dreams? It's fascinating how often it happens.

In order to decode the slang and puns your dream serves up, you'll have to recite your dream out loud and, if you can, get a friend to listen. It does take practice, but you might find that when you're dreaming of trying to get your boyfriend to straighten the walls of a dam, you're actually asking him to be damned straight!

Take time to listen to the words and descriptions you use. Your own words will be tossed back at you with your own amazing unconscious creativity.

Common Dream Themes

You'll find that you're not alone in certain types of dreams. Exam anxiety, for instance, can show up in dreams even when you've been out of school for many years. Dreams about falling, being chased, riding in a car—we share some common themes because we share a common culture. Each theme carries a broad message, but the specifics come to you in your personal code, through the details of the dream. Use these common themes as jumping-off points—but don't stop there. Look at the details of your dream to see what you're trying to tell yourself. (Some dreams incorporate more than one of these common themes, making them more complex and, of course, more interesting.)

Note how the underlying theme of each dream is completely different than the subject of the dream. It's just one more way your unconscious shows you how creative you are.

Common Dream Situations

Theme	*Interpretation*
Transportation, such as cars, bikes, planes, trains, etc.	Where you're headed in waking life
Houses and property	Your health
Body morphing or changing	Changes in your emotions

Theme	*Interpretation*
Exam anxiety	Lack of confidence and control
Being chased	Threats or fears in your life
Falling	Feeling helpless in some part of your life
Being lost	Confusion in waking life
I'm naked!	Vulnerability in waking life
Getting hurt, illness, or death	Emotional problems or changes

Personally Deciphering Common Themes

TRANSPORTATION

Underlying personal theme: Where are you going?

Dream questions: Are you in control? If not, who is? What kind of vehicle are you in? How do you feel? Are you excited about getting to a destination, or are you being taken somewhere unknown?

Life questions: What's going on in your life that might fit this situation? Are there steps you can take to have a say in the direction your life is taking?

HOUSES AND PROPERTY

Underlying personal theme: How is your physical body?

Dream questions: What's the condition of the house or property? Is the place shabby or challenged in some way? Where in the house are you?

Life questions: Examine your health and see how your body might correspond to the dream house. Is there a link between the state of your dream place and how you're feeling physically? Exploring new rooms and beautiful spaces is a good sign—you're opening up to new parts of yourself. Perhaps something is being renovated, as in renewed? Watch out for building or expanding your house, which could mean putting on weight.

BODY MORPHING OR CHANGING

Underlying personal theme: Changes in your emotional state.

Dream questions: What part of your body are you dreaming about? Is it your height (power), chest (heart/love), reproductive area (passion, new feelings)?

Life questions: If you're dreaming of teeth, look into anger and how you're expressing or avoiding it. What can you find in your waking feelings that fits the emotions of this dream?

EXAM ANXIETY

Underlying personal theme: Lacking confidence or feeling out of control.

Dream questions: Are you prepared or unprepared? Are you late? Is this a surprise?

Life questions: What's going on in your life that feels new or challenging? Do you have too many obligations? Are you being "tested" or challenged in your life? Do you feel unprepared for what you're doing in waking life? What can you do to feel more in control of your circumstances?

BEING CHASED

Underlying personal theme: Feeling threatened.

Dream questions: Who or what is pursuing you? Is it a real person, an animal, an imaginary creature? What is the threat? Is it to your body, your family, your property? Do you get hurt, or are you avoiding this pain?

Life questions: Are you feeling threatened, or are you afraid of something or someone in your life? What fear is chasing you? What can you do to confront this threat in your life so that you feel more powerful?

FALLING

Underlying personal theme: Helplessness.

Dream questions: Are you hitting the bottom or just out of control? Is someone or something else involved in your fall?

Life questions: What part of your life feels out of control? Can you go deeper within yourself in waking life to find internal security so you can sustain the unknown?

BEING LOST

Underlying personal theme: Confusion.

Dream questions: Where are you? In limbo? In a house? In familiar surroundings? Are you with someone else? Do you find your way out, or do you wake up still feeling lost?

Life questions: What part of your life feels confusing, and how can you clarify it?

I'M NAKED!

Underlying personal theme: Vulnerability.

Dream questions: Where are you in your dream? Does anyone notice you? What are the reactions of people around you?

Life questions: In what part of your life do you feel exposed or vulnerable? Are there steps you can take to feel more secure?

GETTING HURT, ILLNESS, OR DEATH

Underlying personal theme: Emotional problems or change—whether you like it or not.

Dream questions: Are you hurt, or is someone else? What or who inflicts this pain? Do you recover, or are you left in the moment of pain?

Life questions: What or who is making you feel *emotional* pain? What can you do to let your feelings in waking life come to the surface and heal?

Putting It All Together: Carlos's Dream

I am in Mexico City, driving one of the taxis, a green Volkswagen Bug, and the traffic is, as always, very complicated—the roads are bad, it's hard to navigate. I stop in traffic and a little boy gets into the backseat. He's a scruffy little boy, like the boys who steal or beg back where I come from. I don't know if he's going to rob me or if he is a passenger. I feel angry and also a little bit frightened.

—Carlos, 48

Carlos, a businessman based in Europe, had this dream while he was trying to start up a business with some friends from Mexico. What does this all mean? There are many clues here.

- Taxi: Carlos is driving a car that serves others.
- Bad roads: The situation/path he is on isn't smooth.
- Traffic: There are many distractions and difficulties caused by others.
- Hard to navigate: He doesn't know how to get where he's going.
- Green: He's enclosed in abundance, but it's humble.
- Bug: He's driving a pest around.
- Little boy: There's a part of him that feels young and vulnerable.

- Scruffy: He doesn't feel well-groomed or prepared in this situation.
- Robber or begger: Something is threatening him from the outside.
- Angry and frightened: He's frustrated but still afraid of the circumstances.

Carlos knew his dream reflected his business dealings. He was trying to set up a new business, and one of his friends/business partners wasn't acting in their best interest. Carlos was the "face" of the business, the European representative; the friend had been acting in ways that hindered their business proposition, and Carlos was feeling very conflicted about it. This dream stayed with him for weeks, and he used it to clarify his role and assume more power in the deal. He didn't want to taxi others around who might take advantage of him.

A Last Word on Dream Interpretation

With the tools in this chapter and, if you want to go deeper, the aid of books listed in Additional Reading, you'll have a great handle on your dreams throughout your life. But you do have to keep in mind that you don't know it all, and more important, you don't know what you don't know.

Therapists and psychoanalysts are trained to help you use dreams and your waking life situations in order to break unhealthy patterns or work through difficult issues in your life. Sometimes you need a professional to help you see what's really going on.

You don't know what you don't know. You are limited in how deep you can go into your own dreams.

Your ability to analyze yourself is limited, and the same goes for your dreams. You can't be objective about yourself in waking life, and you can't be objective in dream life either. If you have dreams that you can't decipher or if you want more clarity about your dreams and how they impact your everyday life, you might want to seek professional assistance. Dreams help reveal the source of your feelings and actions, and a professional could help you unearth powerful motivations that might be impeding your ability to achieve personal happiness. The more you know about yourself, the better shot you have at living the life you want.

FIVE

Dreaming for Fun and Adventure

You can go wherever you like in your dreams. You can fly, you can go back in time, you can meet aliens and dance with kings. You can do so much more in your dream life than your waking life. But who does?

We're not taught how to be a daring dreamer, or even to give dreaming much thought. You probably don't even know that you can get better at dreaming. It's a weird idea, to think that you can hone your skills and become better at something you feel you have no control of—but you *can* learn to take your dreams into new territory without too much effort.

Enter the world of lucid dreaming, a dream state

in which you are aware you're dreaming. You have your thinking mind with you, not just your unconscious or subconscious. You're there, fully alert, enjoying the action and even directing it. This is by far one of the most exciting and stimulating dreams you can experience.

Lucid Dreams

Before writing this book, my only experience with lucid dreams was accidental. Most of us have these at some point—typically an unpleasant dream from which we try to wake ourselves. In my early lucid dreams, I would typically attempt to rouse myself by trying to scream. (As you probably know, the muscle paralysis that occurs during dream sleep prevents us from actually screaming.) Those dreams were "amateur" lucid dreams, in which I didn't know that I could be the dream master. I didn't know that the fears I had could have been turned around.

I bet you're nodding your head because you've had the same experience—being in a dream, usually an uncomfortable one, and consciously trying to wake up so that it would end.

In a lucid dream, you have the conscious power to control the action.

Imagine if, in that same state, you could redirect the dream to suit your needs. That's the beauty of consciously dreaming with clarity. You don't have to wake up to be safe and remove the fear or stress; you can turn it around right there in your dream.

What you need to do is to train yourself to recognize you're in a dream and that you're in control of the dream. You are the writer, producer, and director. You are the master of every dream you have. Wouldn't you like to use that power more to your advantage?

The Realms Meet

A lucid dream is actually a clever and delicate balance of your waking and dream states. You're walking a fine line between what you know in daily life and what you can create in dream life. It's very cool and incredibly powerful.

First, melding two states of consciousness gives you, for a few moments, a grasp of how broad and colorful your consciousness can be. In daily life you can't fly or breathe underwater, but you can think and make conscious decisions. In dream life you can fly and breathe underwater, but you're not thinking or making decisions. Now consider being able to do both at the same time. Command yourself to fly. Dive under the water and breathe.

Okay, you're not likely to be flying outside your boyfriend's window in reality, but you will feel how light and agile you are in your dream body, which is akin to your spirit body. You will wake up with this memory and carry the imprint of this experience with you every day—and don't underestimate how profound this is. The euphoria of a lucid dream sticks with you in waking life.

Second, lucid dreams are powerful tools to help you solve problems in your daily life. When your conscious mind is operating in the dream state, you can act out (or, more aptly, "dream out") situations you want to work on in your waking life. Lucid dreams offer the chance to rehearse possibilities, test choices, and explore your power to influence outcomes. Dream reality works hand-in-hand with waking reality. Amplifying your personal power in your dreams will have real effects in your waking life. Waking up with the satisfaction of conquering a fear or a foe makes that day great, and the feeling of power and competence you have in your dream will stay with you in your daily life.

It Works

After working with dreams for months, I finally experienced a certifiable lucid dream in which I consciously controlled the action. It happened almost by accident. I say "almost" because I'd been reading and researching lucid dreams, and I was longing to have one. It felt uncomfortable to write about something I'd never experienced. So my unconscious helped me out.

In the middle of the night my young daughter climbed into bed with me because she had had a bad dream. I fell back to sleep with her and dreamed that I woke up, needing to use the bathroom.

When I got to the bathroom, the toilet looked really different than ours. I walked out of the bathroom and then back in to check, and there it was, this weird toilet. Then I realized—"Oh, my God, this is a dream! I'm dreaming!" I went into the living room and thought to myself, "Now that I know I'm dreaming, what do I do? It's mine to control." I looked at the door leading out of our apartment and didn't feel comfortable walking out. So I flew around the living room once and then stopped. Trying to consider what to do next, I felt my sleeping body pull my dream body back in, and I woke up.

The feeling I had upon waking was totally euphoric. I was so excited and happy at having such an amazing experience. The thrill of controlling a dream feels like an amazing high, but you're not high at all. It's really a sense of well-being and serenity, a peaceful buzz.

It was absolutely fascinating, and flying at will was the most joyful, liberating, and energizing feeling I've had in a dream.

Later that night, having been kicked one too many

times by my sleeping daughter, I dragged myself out of my own bed and collapsed into hers. I fell asleep right away, thinking about my lucid dream and wishing I had been able to prolong it. Again, I slept.

> I woke up and went to the kitchen to make a cup of tea. I noticed something different about the kitchen—not an object this time but the atmosphere, and once again, I found myself in a lucid dream. Again, I went into the living room in my dream. I decided to fly, which I love, and I practiced aerial somersaults. Once again, when I paused to think about what to do next, I felt my physical body pull my dream body back in, and I woke up in my daughter's bed.

These are what lucid dreams are like. At some point in a dream, you realize you're dreaming. If you can grasp the fact that you're in control of the action, you get to choose what to do. If you're in a conflict, you can win it; if you're in a pleasurable state, you can prolong it. In my first few lucid dreams I wasn't practiced enough to conjure an awesome dessert or bring in Justin Timberlake for a chat, but there are no limits to lucid dreams. You only have to practice them and work on making them happen.

Lucid Clues

My first lucid dream is an excellent example of how a dream can give a clue to "wake you up." The weird toilet was the clue to the fact that I was dreaming. You can actually suggest to yourself that some object, gesture, or person will show up in a dream to tell you that you're dreaming. It's a predesigned anchor or symbol that you train yourself to recognize—you design your own clue to wake yourself up. Why I conjured a weird toilet, I don't know, but it was enough for my dream self to realize this wasn't real. In most dreams, I would have accepted this weird bathroom and had some sort of anxiety or reaction that would have taken the dream to another level. Instead, I had the clarity and objectivity to see that this was a clue, that my dream wasn't real but I was thinking and lucid within it. Other lucid dreamers have different dream clues, but for some reason my consciousness chose an object that I couldn't deny was weird.

Your dream clues are probably already anchored in your consciousness. If you've been keeping track of your dreams for interpretation purposes, you have many of your own symbols at your fingertips.

My client Jake told me that he often sees his childhood pet, a black Labrador called Molly, in his dreams. I asked him to use Molly as a lucid clue, a device to wake himself up in his own dream.

Jake called me only days later, thrilled at the way Molly helped him in his dream.

I was walking through a thick forest, and it was starting to rain. I couldn't find my way out, and I felt something bad was going to happen. I saw Molly just ahead of me, and I tried to call out to her. She looked back at me but didn't come running the way she usually does. I'm getting more nervous and exasperated, calling her, chasing her, and fearing the rain is going to clobber me. Suddenly I trip and fall to the ground. I feel Molly licking my ear and nudging me to get up. I feel very annoyed but I turn to look at her and suddenly I realize—"I'm dreaming! This is a dream! I'm 'awake' in the dream." I get up, hug Molly, look around the forest. It smells so good; it's so lush and lovely. I tell Molly to run with me. There's a lake just past the trees, and it's sunny. I'm about to dive into the water and I wake up.

—Jake, 31

Jake was so excited from that dream he called me at the earliest hour he dared the next morning. He couldn't wait to try it again.

You, too, can establish your own clue to the fact that you're dreaming. It's a marker to wake your unconscious self and jar it into using your dream state with intention.

Acquaint yourself with your recurring dream symbols to recognize clues in your dream experience.

Ask for It

You can do it, too, my friend. Yes, you can. You've probably already had those dreams you want to wake up from, those almost-lucid dreams in which you know it's a dream and you want to escape. Now you can actually ask for a lucid dream and, if you're persistent and not just casually playing around, you'll get one.

Achieving a lucid dream is a bit like developing a great tennis serve. The more you try, the better you get.

Get a Clue or a Cue

Yes, you need a clue. It's the easiest way to have a lucid dream. Pick out a gesture, a word, or an object and say to yourself, "If I see this when I'm asleep, I know I'm dreaming." That's your cue.

This takes practice in itself. If you decide a red ball is going to be your cue to wake up in a dream, you still have to notice the red ball. You have to make that connection.

Many of the dream experts who have studied lucid dreaming encourage dreamers to constantly ask, "Is this a dream?" throughout the day. This is a way to program yourself to be more aware when you're actually asleep. My five-year-old daughter is not a scientist, yet she often asks me, "Is this real, or is this a dream?" Not taking my word for it, she jumps up and feels herself hit the ground, then assures herself, "It's real."

If a child can question whether she's awake or dreaming, why can't we? We're just so accustomed to our daily consciousness that we don't even think to test our nighttime awareness.

Try asking yourself if you're awake or dreaming, then take that test to bed with you. If you ask yourself that question when you're dreaming, you might just embark on a real lucid dream.

The Usefulness of Lucidity

Sure, flying in a dream is fun, even euphoric. But is that all there is to it? Not in the least. Lucid dreaming—having the power to redirect the action of your dream—makes you feel stronger and more confident, which actually helps you in your waking life.

If you're being chased by a monster and then realize it's just a dream, you can turn around and pop that monster one right in the nose, then make him leave and go about your business. If you're freaking out over a math test and you realize it's just a dream, tear it up, walk out, and go somewhere fun. You don't have to endure anxiety or fear or anything else unpleasant if you become lucid in a dream. But guess what—this is also great practice for dealing with fear and anxiety in real life.

Taking control in a lucid dream brings you more power to shift circumstances in your waking life. While you can't dictate precisely what happens in your dream, you can create your own safety in any circumstance.

You know that your daily life is reflected in your dream life, but remember that your dream life is reflected in your waking life as well. When you have nightmares, you wake up with the imprint of fear or dread on you. When you have a great dream, you wake up in a good mood, and your waking disposition that day benefits as well.

Taking control, whether it's triumphing in adverse circumstances or simply choosing an enjoyable experience such as flying, can bring you peace, power, and personal satisfaction in your daily life. Now, isn't that appealing?

Not Just Fun

I'm standing in my living room, which is really kind of a country lodge in my dream. There's a beautiful stone fireplace, nice light, a spacious and serene feeling. I see people emerging from another room. They are all very old and they are naked. They walk in a line, calmly, out my front door. I'm a little bit annoyed that these naked people are walking through my nice room, but I don't say anything. Then the atmosphere changes, the room darkens, and I feel a little nervous. I see a dark figure; it seems to be a young man in a black cat suit and black mask. He's prowling the room. I feel a little fear, then something clicks in my brain—"I'm dreaming! I don't have to be afraid." I jump into the air and hang out near the ceiling, like Samantha used to in the old TV show *Bewitched*. The room lightens. The dark figure is sitting on a sofa, looking very comfortable. I point to him and command him to leave. He passes right through the front door. I decide I'm going to use my lucid dream to see what it's like to go through the front door, too. I stick my hand through the door first, to see if my dream body could pass through the "solid" door. It does, and I pass through. It feels like I'm walking through gelatin. It's a little denser than me, but it's easy to move through. I'm out the door now and I'm in a hotel, high up in a tower. I fly down to the ground floor where there is a beautiful restaurant and people are eating, laughing, and talking. I fly around the room a bit and then wake up, back in my bed, in my body, very happy and at ease.

I related this dream to my sister, explaining how wonderful it was to have this kind of lucid dream. I didn't give a thought to the symbolism since I was so taken with the experience itself. She calmly and very accurately pointed out that this dream was about our stepfather's approaching death. I took my sister's point and looked at the dream; it all made sense. It was a delicate emotional time for me; I was trying to give my mother support but not let the situation color my daily life, where taking care of my own family was my priority.

Here's how I interpreted this dream:

The country lodge. This is a nice place to hang out, it's comfortable and spacious. This is me, my "living space," but it's also transient, a "lodge" where other people come and go.

Old people, naked, calmly walking out my door. Vulnerable, old bodies, no longer needed, calmly leaving life. These people weren't sick or unhappy; they were just going about their business—in death. It was an intrusion that they were in my living room, but I didn't intervene.

The atmosphere changes; the dark figure appears. I feel fear and I also realize that I'm dreaming—the dark figure is the clue that wakes me up to "lucidity." I use my lucid state to command this fear figure to leave, and I feel satisfied that I'm in charge.

I pass through the doorway. Using my dream body, I leave my room and see what's out there.

I'm in a hotel, high up in a tower. I'm in a place where people are transient. It's high up, like heaven.

I fly down to a restaurant. People are eating, laughing, and talking. It's life—where people are enjoying themselves. It's where I wake up.

Lucid dreams can come in many forms—you can be in your own space or in some weird, imaginary scenario. The only thing all lucid dreams have in common is that you know you are dreaming. You can direct the action, and you can wake up and interpret the whole thing.

In my dream above, I'm not letting my fear of death, or of my stepfather's death, impede my life. I might be slightly wary of it, but ultimately I recognize that it's just part of life, changing, transient, and not the last step of consciousness—simply the last step of physical reality.

Don't forget to look at your dream symbols once you've had a lucid dream. You can enjoy your dream power and still decode the message your unconscious is sending. Dreams bring on a lot of opportunities to learn!

As your fears decrease in your dream space, they also decrease in your life.

Asking for a Lucid Dream: Incubation

Now that you're all pumped to have a lucid dream, don't wait for one to happen at random. Ask for a lucid dream—ask yourself, that is. Over the ages, dream experts and trained dreamers taught themselves how to guide their own dreams. This technique is called "dream incubation" because you literally nurture the subject and direction of your dream before you get into the dream state. There are many ways to incubate dreams. Ancient dreamers sometimes used psychotropic or hallucinogenic drugs (good for visions, not good for dreams!); some cultures used starvation or harsh deprivation to induce dreams. Other more compassionate cultures simply offered sacred spaces in which dreamers could come and sleep in peace, and dream in a supportive environment. Today it's up to you to induce the dreams you want. Contrary to what you think, it's not that hard and, thank goodness, it does not require any discomfort!

Modern Day Sleep Laboratories

While the ancients once provided sacred space and celebrated important rituals in support of dreams, modern scientific dream studies are conducted in much less sacrosanct environments. Today's sleep labs use electrodes to track REM sleep and more sophisticated electronic equipment to monitor more subtle brain activity. The results are interesting, especially with lucid dreamers. Yet wouldn't the results be even more compelling if dream subjects didn't feel so conscious of being lab rats—watched, measured, and analyzed? The good news is that researchers who study dreams are often test subjects themselves. Hopefully, in their own best interest—and in the interest of their good night's rest—they'll find a better way to study dreams in the lab.

Author and lucid dream expert Dr. Stephen LaBerge offers many ways to attract lucid dreams into your night life. I suggest you try what he calls the WILD method, Wake Initiated Lucid Dreams (in *Exploring the World of Lucid Dreaming*; see Additional Reading). To induce a lucid dream, your intention to have a lucid dream experience must be strong, and you must constantly reinforce the desire to have a lucid dream during the night, when you wake up in between dreams.

Most of us do wake up after dreaming—or at some point in the night—to readjust covers, smooth pillows, or go to the bathroom. When you're in these very peripheral waking states, you're highly suggestible—similar to being under hypnosis. You're not fully awake, ready to start your day, but in a haze. In this state it is very easy to induce a lucid dream. You just have to give yourself a simple reminder. I've been known to mutter, "I want a lucid dream" or simply "Lucid dreams" during the night.

Having used this method successfully, I can tell you that it might make you tired in the morning. Even though you already wake up between dreams, you probably don't remember it. When you use these sleep pauses to prompt lucid dreams, you become more fully roused. You can still go back to sleep, of course, but your dreams are going to be more powerful and more vivid in order to get your attention and wake you up in the dream. I had several colorful dreams before a lucid one, and they took their toll on my rest. It really was dream work! With practice, you don't feel quite as pooped because you don't have to work as hard, but in the beginning this is a very real side effect.

The intention to have a lucid dream is critical. Your conscious and unconscious self must cooperate in order to make this work.

Evolving Lucid Dreams

Lucidity isn't just for facing fears and working things out. More proficient lucid dreamers—those who have had much practice and wake up in dreams more easily—sometimes go beyond their own ego issues into a spiritual experience.

This has nothing to do with religion, although you can shift it that way if you like. Once you are lucid in a dream and, if you need to, work out the fear or the problem that your dream has presented to you, you can stay in that lucid dream and meditate. Ask for spirit to join with you. Call out to angels, energy, God, whatever you want, to join with your dreaming self, and you will experience infinite love and compassion.

This is a connection between you and spirit that has nothing to do with your personality or your body—it's more like the umbilical cord that attaches your soul to the Greater Energy of the universe. This feeling is most often achieved through meditation, but it can come to you in a dream.

Imagine a lucid dream in which you call out to spirit for healing, or simply to experience some divine energy.

It's amazing. It's healing. And it requires practice!

Making It Last

You'd think that once you had control of your dream, you'd be able not only to direct it but to keep it going for as long as you like. Sadly, this isn't the case. The more practiced you get at lucid dreaming, the longer you'll be able to sustain it, but eventually you'll feel your body pull you back and you're done. It's over, and you were just getting started!

I have found that trying to control the dream *too* much brings it to an end. It's a delicate balance, this combination of waking mind and dream state—a blend of two realms that aren't accustomed to being together. Of course, the more you blend them the easier it gets.

Once the action in your dream dies down a bit and you have time to think, you'll start to tip the balance back to your physical, waking reality. Anytime you pause for more than a moment to ask yourself, "Now what do I do?" you lean away from your dream state.

Some lucid dreamers distract themselves by falling down or spinning to keep their dream state active. You'll find your own way when you get to this point. It's always amusing to see how long you can maintain a lucid dream, and you'll be challenging yourself again and again to make it last longer.

Is This for Real?

Even if you've read as many books about dreams and psychic phenomena as I have, you may be raising one eyebrow, wondering if this is really possible. Sure, you've had dreams in which you *knew* you were dreaming, but can you really take control of them, can you really be conscious in a dream? Somewhere in your heart, you know you can.

LaBerge tested the validity of lucid dreams by finding a way for the dreamer to communicate with the sleep lab. Using specific eye movements during REM sleep, the dreamer could signal the sleep lab that he was awake in his dream. The experiment has been repeated many times with many subjects, and it has been shown that you can be conscious in a dream and communicate back to the waking world.

Further research in this area suggests that you can dream physiological changes into being. One of the first tracked was that of sexual response. Several lucid dreamers agreed to bring themselves to orgasm in a dream. Recordings of their physical activity and muscular responses correlated with their claims that they climaxed in their dreams. Why do you care? Because once you've got your lucid dreaming down, you can plan a dream date with that special guy and not have to worry about birth control.

Many psychiatrists, psychologists, and sleep experts are exploring how lucid dreams might actually help us in our daily lives. Someone who's anemic might dream that her red blood cells were plentiful and strong. Now take it a step further—what if that lucid dream of healthy red blood cells actually helped *create* healthy red blood cells? Could we dream our way to health?

It's possible.

Stick to It

Don't get frustrated if you aren't able to experience a lucid dream right away. It's not that easy to crack the code of your unconscious. But once you do, you'll never want to go back.

Skillful dreaming takes practice, and you get it every night! Just pay attention—remember to ask for a lucid dream (*intend* to wake up in your dreams) and take advantage of your power when you are, indeed, awake.

You have a lifetime of dreaming ahead of you. Imagine the possibilities.

SIX

Dreaming for Answers: The Psychic Power of Dreams

We've already covered a great deal of dream space. Simply remembering and interpreting dreams can take a lifetime of dedication and learning. Moving into lucid dreams creates yet another, deeper dream experience that adds an extra dimension to your nighttime self. The possibilities at the lucid dream stage are already overwhelming. Imagine moving deeper, further into dream space. Get ready!

Once again, your dreams will be made up of familiar symbols and archetypes—your dream language. But the messages, the answers, the ideas—these will come not from your unconscious alone but from the many realms of consciousness that can join you in your sleep state.

Dreams are clothed in a reality you can recognize, but they aren't confined to your own imagination.

Dreams are your connection to an unbounded territory of power and healing. Your dreams span many different planes of awareness and encompass much more than your own little mental territory.

Of course, we all think that our imaginations are pretty wild, but let me assure you that they're nothing compared to the whole wacky universe. When you dream, your waking life personality, that self-editor and cultural screener, takes a big backseat to the energies and influences of the dream realms. You're much more open to ideas, possibilities, and expansion when your waking mind isn't telling you to remember to pick up your dry cleaning or that you can't possibly see Great Aunt Flo because she's been dead for years. Your dream space gives you more scope, more flexibility to find answers and to explore ideas.

And most of us sorely underutilize this amazing power.

Your Dream Skills

Your ability to access that kind of profound dream and to be open to its meaning has a lot to do with your personality and beliefs. Are you very rigid? Do you think that reality is limited to the here and now? Or do you allow that there are other realms of energy, that your spirit isn't confined to your body, that there are many dimensions of consciousness?

If you're very measured or inflexible in your beliefs and ideas, if your world is limited to what you can see and prove, you're not going to have as much opportunity for great dream experience as those who are open to new ways of thinking, believing, and living. It's unlikely that a closed mind in waking life will have great success reaching different realms of consciousness in the dream state. You're only as open as you permit yourself to be; so if you want to rethink your beliefs, now is a good time to start.

For those of you who already "get" that our physical bodies and our lives are only a temporary stop on a greater path, you're in good shape to dream for answers. Dreaming is another reality for you, a place where you can try out new experiences and even take them back with you to the daytime world.

Afraid of conflict? In your dreams you can conquer whomever you choose. Shy? In your dreams you can be outgoing and open. Stumped on some problem? Dreams can get you thinking in more productive directions.

Dream space can be an avenue of great richness, full awareness, and flourishing creativity. This very real part of you feeds and informs your waking life.

In a single night, you can explore several different dream spaces, experimenting with realities and chaotic creativity.

Advanced Dreaming

First, take a moment to evaluate how ready and open you are to our next dream territory.

- Are you interested in examining your own motivations and issues?
- Do you believe that your consciousness can span more than your waking personal life?
- Have you meditated or prayed and felt yourself open into a more expansive energy?

The more open you are, the more opportunity you'll have to dream through realms of broader experience, to use what we call psychic or intuitive dreams. Your dream body can take you places you've never known in life. Beyond dream interpretation, beyond lucidity—get on your magic carpet and enjoy the ride.

The Stuff of Dreams: Converging Realms

Dreams are a cooperative enterprise. Your unconscious self is not creating your dream alone. We briefly touched on how, in dream time, you open yourself up to realms of energy, creativity, and consciousness that converge for your personal use. This, in part, is how you can derive dream answers to waking life questions. This is also how you can visit people and places that are not available to you in your waking life. Try to grasp how profound and amazing this is! Frankly, it's as impossible to understand as the concept of infinity, but once you get the gist of how enormous your dream space can be, you'll want to use it more consciously, enthusiastically—and more often!

Are you wondering what I really mean by "realm"? I like the analogy of the electromagnetic spectrum, which represents all of the different kinds of energy we can measure.

The electromagnetic waves we can see with the naked eye are those that create color. But that's only a small slice of the spectrum; most of it is invisible, from gamma rays at the highest frequency to radio waves at the lowest. Visible light, the part that we see, falls within a very narrow band in this vast spectrum.

Think of our lives, our consciousness, as one narrow band or frequency in the spectrum of all consciousness, all intelligence, all energy. Our reality is a tiny sliver of all that energy. It's the only realm we can see, but our waking lives are only one wavelength of the energy that represents all of life.

When you're dreaming, you can more easily access different parts of the vast spectrum of consciousness. You're not confined to a physical body. Your energy is more fluid, so it can join or touch upon other realms. I don't know how far you can go into these realms, but I suspect you can go anywhere you want. Dreaming, especially skillful dreaming, gives you many more options than you have in daily life.

In your dreams you are much more open to the energies that provide psychic information. You don't screen what comes to you, and you don't tell yourself what's "real." These psychic realms, which I imagine to be like energetic intelligence, can hook up with your dream space to give you access to ideas that aren't native to your consciousness. You can literally get input from infinite layers of spiritual energy and add to your knowledge and awareness.

The more your consciousness opens, the broader your spectrum and the more you can use in your life, both waking and dreaming.

This isn't to say being awake separates you from the other realms completely. You can access various realms through meditation, prayer, and other means in waking life, especially with practice. But in sleep we all have more agility, whether we're skillful or not.

You have enormous creativity at your disposal in dream time. If you're interested in things you can't explore in your daily life, do it in dreams. The more skillful you get at dreaming, the more satisfying your dreams become. It's an amazing thing, to traverse the realms of consciousness. And you do it every night, already, without even knowing it.

Big Questions, Big Answers

Your dreams are already giving you a lot of answers and plenty to think about, but if you're really in need of specific advice, you can turn to your dreams for help. Ask for an answer, and you'll receive one. Of course, you can't precisely script a dream. But you can program it, the way you'd set up your preferences on a computer. To do this we're going to use dream incubation, discussed in the last chapter, in a very specific way.

Through dream incubation, you're going to plug into different creative realms to help you work through a problem. Scientists have been known to come up with solutions and breakthroughs in their dreams; writers find inspiration; artists cross into new territory. You, too, can "sleep on it" and ask your dreams to help you figure out issues in your love life, your work life, your family. You can even ask the spirit realms to come and teach you things or resolve your differences with someone who is not alive anymore.

But remember, even skillful dreams come in weird disguises. You'll have to interpret the dream to get those answers.

I learned to meditate out of sheer frustration with my job. I was under too much stress when

I worked as a trader on the floor of the Exchange. I longed for something more meaningful, and I was working on some kind of career change. I didn't know what to do next, but when I meditated I felt that a change was at least possible. I felt less oppressed, less hopeless. Then a friend told me about dream incubation, asking for a dream to figure out where my career could go next. I had this dream.

I am sitting in my apartment, a basement apartment that looked out into a garden. The room is filled with natural light and it's a nice atmosphere. I'm at ease, but I'm hot. I open the window that looks out into the garden, and I see lots of kittens. Some jump into my room, and I'm happy to see them. More jump in. They are soft and clean, playful and sweet. I'm feeling curious as to why so many kittens are here, but I'm not afraid or anxious. I wake up in my real apartment, wondering what those kittens were all about.

—Rose, 36

Answers Take Time

Rose first noted that this dream took place in a basement, the inner and deeper part of herself. The room was light, so she wasn't in the dark or afraid, and it looked onto a garden, which Rose took as a symbol for abundance. Those cats played a big part of her dream. What could they be?

Cats, traditionally, stand for mystical wisdom (see Chapter Four) and kittens are youthful and playful. Putting those ideas together, Rose interpreted the animals in her dream as standing for new creative ideas, new ways to approach work—and lots of them!

While this wasn't a clear-cut answer to what she should do next, Rose was so intrigued that she devoted herself to studying dream interpretation and eventually found herself drawn to working with healing. She left her job and studied to be a certified massage therapist. On the side, her interest in dream symbols and the stars led her to study astrology. She's also currently working on a book. Those are numerous creative projects, loaded with mystical wisdom. Rose's dream was another example of how the answer is there, buried in the symbols.

Asking for an Answer: More Dream Incubation

The easiest way to find an answer through your dreams is to ask for it. No kidding. Just state your desire for an answer. Say it out loud, just before you go to sleep. It works like a hypnotic suggestion. Ask about anything—your next haircut, your spirit guides, what it's like to be a guy—the dream world is open to everything. For example, "Tonight I dream about the man I'm going to marry, and when I wake up, I remember this dream" or, "Tonight I dream about finding a new home, and when I wake up, I remember my dream." You won't know what you're going to get until you wake up, and even then it's not going to be something you understand right away.

You will remember your answer dream, but you won't know what it means until you let it digest a while. Record it. Listen to yourself recite it out loud. Remember how you felt in the dream. All that work you did in the previous chapter comes in handy now.

Tips for Receiving Dream Answers

State what you want to dream about out loud.

Always use the present tense.

State that you want to remember your dream.

Record your dream when you wake up.

Some dreamers get their information in the middle of the night, so be warned. You might be waking up at 3 A.M. from a vivid dream—that's your dream answer, my friend. You have to rouse yourself enough to record the dream or you'll lose some valuable information. I can't tell you how often I wake up and the clock says exactly 3 A.M. or maybe a few minutes off. Then, of course, I have to wake up just enough to get the dream down on paper, or think about it enough to keep it fresh for the morning.

It's actually very common to have your answer dreams arrive during this inconvenient hour. The deeper night hours, or, to be more accurate, the early morning hours, seem to be closer to the creative realms. It's easier to receive and intuit information in dreams around that time of night. Occasionally, however, your most significant dream is the last dream you have right before you wake up, so make sure your alarm clock isn't going to spoil it.

For a good night's rest, you can also state that you wake up rested and refreshed, no matter how little you sleep.

Dreaming for answers requires patience and commitment. Both are easily disregarded when it's time to go to bed. If you're tired or distracted, it's hard to remember to state your desire correctly. Then, of course, you have to remember your dreams and decode them for the answers that lie buried in your dreamscape.

Stay with the process. Be consistent, and the answers will come.

SEVEN

Deeper Dreams and Psychic Experience

The Future and You

You dream of the future a lot. You may not think you do, but haven't you ever had déjà vu, the feeling that you've already lived a certain moment?

We *all* dream of future events—some trivial, some momentous—because dream time is dynamic, creative, and, get this: there is no time in dream space.

We're heading into some choppy waters now, because any discussion of time gets a little hard to swallow. Try on this idea, though: time is linear in waking life only because we want it to be. Time isn't sequential, progressive, or consecutive in the dream realm or in any other manifestation of spiritual energy. We have our nice little time-keeping procedures to keep us sane, to make sense of our physical reality. Sure, you get born, you age, you die; but what we trust to be time and the passing of time is only a way to make sense of waking life. It keeps us feeling safe when we can predict the passage of time. Yet time is actually very elastic, and also simultaneous. What has passed and what is to come is all here right now. (Feeling seasick yet?) Time is like spirit: infinite, endless, and constant. What seems to be in the past is still with us now. What seems to be in the future exists now as well. It's all part of a whole.

I know, I know—you're going to argue that the future isn't predestined, so how could it already exist? I agree, we live in a realm of free will. We choose to make our future. Yet, even though the future is constantly shifting, it always exists. Our past, our current actions, our choices every single second, influence what the future is at this very moment. Just because it hasn't manifested yet doesn't mean it doesn't exist somewhere on some energetic level. This is why you can influence the future, you can form the future—you can *change* the future. But it exists right now, in whatever form the choices and beliefs of this moment dictate.

Since it's impossible to conceive of the simultaneity of time and stay sane, look at it another way. Time is clearly not an accurate or constant measure. Spend fifteen minutes in a doctor's office and it might seem like an entire day. Spend fifteen minutes reading e-mail and it goes by in a blink. Time feels different because it *is* different.

Dreams that contain the most amazing, complicated, difficult, and lengthy plots might take only a matter of minutes to dream. The action in your dream may have taken hours in your dream because your dream space doesn't keep time the way your clock does.

Dreams that take you into future events can do so because those events have already formed in dream space. Your dreams are constantly trying to "wake you up" to your own psychic power. You dream you're crossing a certain street with a certain person and you're talking about a great meal you've had, then a few days or weeks later this precise situation occurs, down to the last word. You walk across that same street, with that same person, you say those same things and—*poof!*—

you realize you've done this before, in a dream. Yikes.

Bear in mind that you don't have to completely understand the fluidity of time or how you can dream the future and live it days later. You only need to know that it's true, that time is very flexible, so that you can make the most of your advanced dreaming skills.

Dream Blueprints: Advanced Future Forming

Not only can you ask to dream for an answer about your life; you can also dream to create a new path or forge ahead in new directions by starting the process first in your dreams. This takes a great deal of commitment and consistency, though, so if you're a shirker, it won't work.

In this advanced dream state you can ask yourself to use your dream space to create or attract something you want in your life. You have to be pretty specific, and again, consistent—almost persistent—to get this baby going. State what you want to do aloud and in the present tense. For example,

Tonight I dream about my next creative project, the focus of this project, how I engage in it, the people involved, the feeling, the smell, even the taste of what this project is. And I wake up rested and remember this dream.

This technique is called "creating a seed form" or a "psychic blueprint." Since we've already agreed on the fluidity of time, you'll understand how you can literally plant energy in the dream realm, continuously feed it, then have it "meet" you in your "real" or physical reality. This process requires consistency; every time you conjure this seed form in your dream state, you're adding more to its energy. The more energy you add, the more power it has to manifest. The idea of what you're going to do doesn't sit only in the realm of imagination. It is also born from various creative realms, intelligence, and spiritual energy. You'll be piecing your seed form together with the help of infinite resources.

Using the seed form method, you'll be bringing your dream life and your waking life closer together. This is a good thing—don't worry, it's not a combination that creates anything weird. You'll be more likely to access all that wild creativity of the dream state while you're still walking around, rationally operating in your waking life. It makes you more creative, agile, and alert.

None of this, by the way, happens in an obvious, cut-and-dried fashion. Nope. Working with dreams and seeing results in your waking life creates a blur of action and response. You don't actually see it coming, but you arrive at the place you've created with the help of your dreams without noticing the road that led you there.

It takes time to build that seed form. The more you do it the better it gets. The more energy and dream time you put into it, the more power you'll have in your waking life to get there. Eventually you'll be in that new creative project or that new relationship, and you will look back and realize that you created it all by yourself (with the help of your dreams, the universe, and trust in the infinite creative realms).

This is the place where you can actually make your dreams come true.

A word on reality here, though. Plant seed forms for things you want to achieve or create in your life *that are actually doable*. Not to limit you, but please, being "discovered" by a modeling agent? What you want to create should be within the realm of possibility. Be honest with yourself. How about creative success in your career? You'll get better results with things that are more realistically available.

Spiritual Work in Dream Time

Of course it's cool to create things in your life through your dreams. But you can also use your dreams to do deeper spiritual work, address karmic issues, and open to healing. Did you know you could go so deep while still enjoying some romping and canoodling dreams? You sure can! (But probably not on the same night.)

> I was going through a very hard time in my life when I had this dream. My grandmother, with whom I'd been very close, had just died, my love life had evaporated—I was feeling lost.
>
> I dream that I am walking with my grand-

mother in the desolate snowy tundra in Alaska. I am very tired. A man approaches us, a native in some sort of ritual dress. At first I don't take any notice of him, but he walks up to us and tells me he is going to kill us. I am now afraid. He tells me that if I kill my grandmother, he'll spare me. My grandmother pleads with me to kill her so that I can live. The man gives me a knife, and I weep as I stab my grandmother in the heart. She dies instantly, and I fall over her body sobbing. Suddenly I am standing and my grandmother is embracing me. Over and over again she says, "I forgive you, I love and I forgive you," which makes me cry even more. I turn to the man, and he raises the knife. I cry out, but he stabs me and kills me. I'm angry as I die—he had promised that he wouldn't kill me, but he did it anyway. I die, and the most extraordinary feeling comes over me. I float in the most amazing light, like streaks of a gorgeous sunset—reds, oranges, yellows, magnificent. I am no longer crying. I feel joy, peace, and light. I wake up.

—Lynn, 29

This was a profound dream for Lynn. While she was open to spiritual teachings and was meditating regularly, Lynn had to take some time to decipher what this dream was about. Here's how she went about interpreting the dream:

Walking in Alaska. I felt lost in a harsh environment. When I thought about Alaska, I recalled lyrics from a song I learned in summer camp as a child:

What's your name, little girl?
"My name is Alaska."
Alaska What, little girl?
"I'll ask my mommy."

I immediately think that's a dream pun; I'm a little girl, and I need to "ask my mommy" who I am.

The man in native dress arrives. To me, a man in a native costume is someone who knows ancient rituals and secrets. He's calm, not mean—dispassionate, powerful. He's a piece of history, not a real person.

My grandmother pleads for me to kill her. I'm in a terrible state, but I follow her instructions. She is sacrificing herself for my sake. Her love is so great.

I kill her. This is horrible. I have to do it, but I still can feel the horror of this action. My grandmother is only recently deceased, and she feels very real to me in this dream. I can still feel the pain of that.

She forgives me. Suddenly she's not dead, and she's holding me and telling me she loves me. It's such profound forgiveness and emotion it makes me feel even more sadness. I almost can't take in all of her love. It's bigger than me. I force myself to open to love.

He stabs me, and I'm angry as I die. I'm so angry that I complied with his wishes and killed my grandmother, but I still die. I feel duped. I followed his instructions, and I still got killed. He isn't angry or scary, though. He's just this old man who stabs me. It feels like he has a purpose he has not revealed. He is both ancient wisdom and the deceit of life. He makes me think of male bosses and boyfriends who lie to make it easier on themselves but do bad things behind my back.

I feel the extraordinary lightness of death. My anger quickly releases as I feel uplifted and joyful in death. I no longer feel sadness or pain, only happiness and light. This feeling is supremely healing. I love being "dead." Letting go was an amazing experience. I was bummed out when I woke up.

Lynn's Dream Shaman

This dream hit Lynn right between the eyes. The dream came at a time of great personal turmoil, and the dream is still vivid to her today, ten years later. Lynn knew right away that the dream was symbolically about leaving behind her life as a "little girl," but she felt there was more to it.

The old native man, her grandmother—these people were symbols of ancient wisdom, *those who have come before us*. The man was the dispassionate shaman, the mysterious medicine man who doesn't disclose his purpose but nonetheless carries out the necessary ritual. He embodied the masculine archetype in its basic, patriarchal detachment. The grandmother, aside from being the healing, loving, and compassionate feminine archetype, represents the crone, the female embodiment of wisdom. Lynn chose to listen to these beings and even felt betrayed by the man, yet she surrendered, ultimately, to her higher self. Is this a significant dream?

Yes. Some experts would interpret this as a shamanistic journey, in which Lynn undertook a terrible task, died, and was reborn. Surrender, forgiveness, and redemption were all major turning points in this dream. Lynn hadn't just had a dream; she'd undergone an ancient ritual.

Healing Beings and Teachers

Lynn's dream is just one of many examples of evolved beings living a part of life in dream space. The man in native dress who "killed" both Lynn and her grandmother wasn't just a dream image from Lynn's psyche. He was a real visitor to Lynn's dream realm, a being who came to initiate these actions and allow Lynn to react with both her waking mind—the part suffering from the loss of her grandmother—and her dream self, who was able to perform a heinous act of murder and to die and be reborn. Lynn's dream was actually a spiritual test.

Be on the lookout for healers and teachers in your own dreams. The whole concept of these beings is somewhat lost on us, now that we're trained to think of teachers as people in classrooms. But in fact the dream realm is heavily populated by teachers and guides who work with you even when you don't recognize them. If you do have a dream that feels important and has a big impact on your life, you've probably been touched by a guide.

You can call guides into your dream life by asking for them, just the way you conduct dream incubation. Add a line for them in your dream blueprint.

> *Tonight I dream about moving to a new city. I dream of the feel and vitality of this city. I dream of my prosperity and health in this new place. I call in a dream guide to accompany me in the dream and to teach me what I need to know. I wake up refreshed, and I remember this dream.*

Don't give up if you don't have an immediate and obvious answer to your dream request. Guides will work with you on many dreams. You will not necessarily remember your dream consciously, but a dream teacher or guide will begin to work with you if you consistently ask for it. They'll reveal themselves in time, when you're ready. Like everything else, it takes practice.

What Lynn Found Out

The point of Lynn's dream was spiritual progress, accessing her intuition, understanding her psychic power and how she fits into the universe as a healing being, an active participant.

These spiritually profound dreams most often leave the impression that we are supported and loved from beyond this world. When Lynn died in her dream, all of her fears and anger simply evaporated.

That feeling stays with her to this day. Lynn is a perfectly normal working mother with a regular life. But she insists that death doesn't scare her and that she has, since that dream, a new perspective on life. She sees things in a larger framework and has, as she puts it, more "contentment." Lynn is more grounded and more powerful as a result of this one dream.

I know several other people who have experienced profound spiritual connections in their dreams. Beings such as angels, animals, wise women, even alien life-forms have shown up as guides. Be open to yours—you never know what form they will take.

The Psychic Dream Network

Before September 11, 2001, as well as before other major disasters, many people dreamed of something sinister or disastrous happening. Most dreams weren't literal depictions of the actual events, but many were close. In the Introduction, you read about Danielle's dream the day before the terrorists crashed into the World Trade Center. Many people, including me, had premonitions in their dreams about this tragedy. But what good is having such a premonition? What can you do about that?

It may seem like nothing can be done with a disaster dream. First of all, how do you know if it's really a premonition or just your unconscious working out something in your life? Well, you can take steps to find out, by talking to other dreamers. Set up your own dream network with your friends or family members who take dreaming seriously.

By sharing your dream, you'll encourage others to do the same. You'll be able to help one another with interpretation, too. Your friends are more objective and may interpret *your* dreams more readily, and you can do the same for them. My friend Shakira recently had a disaster dream, and she called me up very concerned that another attack on the United States was coming. I gave her dream some thought and then reminded her that she'd taken to calling her boss bin Laden. She laughed and immediately relaxed. Her dream was work related, not a premonition of terrorism.

Let's say you've shared a disturbing dream with a friend, and your friend says, "That's so weird. I had a dream like that, too." Uh-oh. Now what? Keep sharing—keep asking if anyone else had this dream.

Hop online and see if you have company. There are plenty of Web sites on the Internet for dream sharing. Check out the e-zine *Electric Dreams*, available at www.dreamgate.com, where people around the world can share their dreams for both literary experience (you know how hard it is to articulate your dreams!) and for feedback regarding interpretation.

Dream sharing, contrary to what some might think, is an honorable hobby that can be healing for you and the planet. Unlike the dreams your friends might tell you (those long self-aggrandizing adventures), dream sharing yields intelligence about our future.

You can use your dreams to create an alternate reality. If you've had a premonition dream, it doesn't have to come true, especially when you have help from a network of dreamers.

You can use this information to help change the world.

Averting Disaster: Dreams of Peace

Since you're now an advanced experienced dreamer, you're ready to incubate dreams about things other than your next date or when you're going to get a raise. Sure, you can still do this (by all means, use your dreams for your own specific purpose!), but beyond that you can move into the world, helping create the potential reality of peace, harmony, and acceptance.

The dream world supports the physical world. Many people dreaming of peace will increase the possibility for peace.

Using your dreams to make the world a better place might seem a bit odd, but consider the fact that when you're dreaming, your energy is exposed to the greater energy—that vast spectrum of consciousness. You can't get connected to the realms as easily when you're awake, but in dreams you can travel and connect beyond your personal knowledge and experience. Remember, this is how people who have died can contact you, and this is how you can move through time in your dreams. Putting these factors together creates the unique opportunity for you to make an impact on what will be happening in the world and how it happens.

Group Incubation

If you're feeling a little overwhelmed or aghast at the responsibility for single-handedly dreaming about world peace, fear not. You're not alone. The power to shift our world and to make that peace happen must be a group effort. Consciousness—spiritual energies—in all realms are trying to bring about peace on our planet.

Your contribution, your own efforts, add to this energy and make it even more effective.

There are many formal and informal dream co-ops that are already seeking to achieve peace. Check out World Dreams Peace Bridge (www.worlddreamspeacebridge.org) on the Internet. You'll be gratified to know that you're not alone in your curiosity or your desire to make a difference. There is a large community of dreamers out there, ready to welcome you as part of the ongoing effort to create peace on this planet.

When you think you're getting dreams warning of more terrorism, what better time is there to start dreaming for peace?

The Dreams You Don't Know About

In non-REM sleep, when scientists *used to* say you're not dreaming, there's actually something special going on. Recently, brain activity—very low-level brain activity—has been detected during non-REM sleep. Why is this significant? Because it lends credibility to the theory that in all phases of sleep you're connecting to the realms. You're not just killing time between dreams. You're actually getting recharged, both physically and spiritually.

Profound healing takes place during non-REM sleep. You won't remember it. You don't have to—it's a connection of pure energy, of pure spirit.

The time between dreams is a time of white light, of connection to the infinite energy of spirit, a subject that can't be contemplated or explained with your rational mind.

In sleep, you're doing a lot of spiritual work. Hard to believe, isn't it? But your sleep body—your spirit body—is getting recharged. It's the daytime of your soul.

> *The sleep time between periods of REM sleep is still dream time, but one of clear, pure energy. It is an infusion of spiritual source energy.*

In dream and nondream time, "white light" time, your energy is reaffirmed, your purpose is supported, your spirit experiences healing. The world of dreaming and sleep is one of possibilities and connections. It's not nothingness. Quite the contrary—the world of dreaming and sleep is an open forum of creativity and exploration.

You can actually increase your access to this clear, pure energy by stating your desire for it. Just as in any dream incubation, go to sleep with the intention to connect to healing energy. In your REM sleep and again in between, in those nonmemorable rest phases, your request for source energy will be honored. You will be joining the realms with your specific purpose, and great healing can take place on all levels.

The Dream of Our Reality

The more you play with your dreams, explore them and understand them, the more your life will unfold into the dimensions of pleasure and joy you seek.

It's an amazing tapestry of experience: dreams taken into daily life, daily life taken into dreams. As the gap between your physical world and your dream world narrows, the possibilities for your happiness expand.

Our reality is, in part, created by our dreams. As you consciously explore your dream world, as you express yourself in dream language and interpret it, you evolve. But there's more: your personal experience is a part of the greater world, and your desire to understand yourself and your dream world has only positive effects on those around you.

As you work with your dreams, don't be afraid to share the thrill with those you love. Get others to dream with you—see if you can meet your friends in your dreams. I know people who do this regularly!

Your dreams and the dreams of your loved ones are important components in shaping our world. Don't be afraid to get more involved. It's an easy, regular gig—you do sleep every night, right?

And do not for a minute think that using your dreams for personal gain is not in line with spirit. Your satisfaction with life is important. It contributes to the world's positive vibes and is healing for everyone. It's fine to be selfish in your dreams; so don't be shy. Personal happiness is a spiritual pursuit.

Sweet Dreams

Yes, it's time to hit the sack. Now every time you go to sleep, you'll know that you're not exactly wasting time on your back. Of course, you don't have to dream consciously every night. You can leave that TV on when you feel like it. You can eat spicy food and have nightmares. It won't take away from all the knowledge you now possess for how to work with your dreams.

When you feel like it, keep a journal. Create your own dream network. You can do so much for your own life as well as the lives of others if you take the time to use your dreams.

To start, use the Dream Worksheets on the following pages to make notes about the dreams you remember. You have a lifetime of dreaming ahead of you—it's so easy. Nighty-night . . . and get to work!

Dream Worksheets

Dream Worksheet

Dream Title:

Date:

Action (present tense):

Main Symbols:

Elements

Colors

Numbers

People

Places

Puns

Action

Emotion You Felt

Personal Interpretation:

Notes:

Dream Worksheet

Dream Title:

Date:

Action (present tense):

Main Symbols:

Elements

Colors

Numbers

People

Places

Puns

Action

Emotion You Felt

Personal Interpretation:

Notes:

Dream Worksheet

Dream Title:

Date:

Action (present tense):

Main Symbols:

Elements

Colors

Numbers

People

Places

Puns

Action

Emotion You Felt

Personal Interpretation:

Notes:

Dream Worksheet

Dream Title:

Date:

Action (present tense):

Main Symbols:

Elements

Colors

Numbers

People

Places

Puns

Action

Emotion You Felt

Personal Interpretation:

Notes:

Dream Worksheet

Dream Title:

Date:

Action (present tense):

Main Symbols:

Elements

Colors

Numbers

People

Places

Puns

Action

Emotion You Felt

Personal Interpretation:

Notes:

Dream Worksheet

Dream Title:

Date:

Action (present tense):

Main Symbols:

Elements

Colors

Numbers

People

Places

Puns

Action

Emotion You Felt

Personal Interpretation:

Notes:

Dream Worksheet

Dream Title:

Date:

Action (present tense):

Main Symbols:

Elements

Colors

Numbers

People

Places

Puns

Action

Emotion You Felt

Personal Interpretation:

Notes:

Dream Worksheet

Dream Title:

Date:

Action (present tense):

Main Symbols:

Elements

Colors

Numbers

People

Places

Puns

Action

Emotion You Felt

Personal Interpretation:

Notes:

Dream Worksheet

Dream Title:

Date:

Action (present tense):

Main Symbols:

Elements

Colors

Numbers

People

Places

Puns

Action

Emotion You Felt

Personal Interpretation:

Notes:

Additional Reading

The Seth Material by Jane Roberts

Seth Speaks by Jane Roberts

Creative Dreaming by Patricia Garfield

The Universal Dream Key by Patricia Garfield

Exploring the World of Lucid Dreaming by Stephen LaBerge and Howard Rheingold

Lucid Dreaming by Stephen LaBerge and Howard Rheingold

Dreamwork for the Soul by Rosemary Ellen Guiley

www.dreamtree.com

Photo by Tamara Schlesinger

Barrie Dolnick is a former Madison Avenue advertising executive and the author of the Simple Spells book series. She is also a high-profile consultant whose company, Executive Mystic, uses alternative information techniques, including tarot cards, astrology, meditation, and spell casting to guide clients on a successful path. For more information, log on to www.BarrieDolnick.com.